The Achievement Factory

How to Fulfill Your Dreams and Make Life an Adventure

Andrii Sedniev

The Achievement Factory

How to Fulfill Your Dreams and Make Life an Adventure

Published by Andrii Sedniev

Copyright © 2014 by Andrii Sedniev

ISBN 978-1-49955-119-8

First printing, 2014

All rights reserved. No part of this book may be reproduced in any form or by any electronic or mechanical means including information storage and retrieval systems – except in the case of brief quotations in articles or reviews – without the permission in writing from its publisher, Andrii Sedniev.

www.AndriiSedniev.com

PRINTED IN THE UNITED STATES OF AMERICA

Dedications

This book and my love are dedicated to Olena, my wife and partner, who makes every day in life worthwhile. Thank you for supporting me on every stage of development of *The Achievement Factory* and giving encouragement when I needed it the most. Without you, this book might never have been finished.

I also want to dedicate this book to all past students of *The Achievement Factory* who by their success inspire me to become a better person every day.

Contents

INTRODUCTION 1

HAPPINESS 2
    HAPPINESS THEORY 2
    3 KEYS TO AN EXCITING LIFE 5

YOUR LIFE IS IN YOUR HANDS 8
    SELF-RESPONSIBILITY FOR YOUR LIFE 8
    BELIEVE THAT YOU CAN AND WILL ACHIEVE A GOAL 10
    COMMITMENT TO ACHIEVE A GOAL 12

CREATE A DREAM LIST 15
    ALLOW YOURSELF TO DREAM AND HAVE A DESIRE 15
    100 DREAMS EXERCISE 16

PRIORITIZATION 23
    PRIORITIZE GOALS AND BE READY TO PAY THE PRICE 23
    3 SUPER-PRODUCTIVITY QUESTIONS 26

HOW TO SET GOALS 28
    SPECIFIC AND MEASURABLE GOAL 28
    SET ACHIEVABLE GOALS 31

3 TIMEFRAMES FOR GOALS 33
    CREATE A COMPELLING VISION 33
    PROCESS GOALS 34
    SET A TASK FOR A DAY 36

VISUALIZATION 39
    WHAT IS VISUALIZATION? 39
    BENEFITS OF VISUALIZATION 40

VISUALIZATION MAGIC FORMULA 43

POSITIVE THINKING 46

LAW OF ATTRACTION 46
PUT YOUR BRAIN ON A POSITIVE DIET 47
ELIMINATE NEGATIVE THOUGHTS 52

STRATEGY 58

A PLAN FOR ACHIEVING A GOAL 58
MEASURE PROGRESS 60
A PERFECT STRATEGY IS A FLEXIBLE STRATEGY 62
ONE STEP CLOSER TO THE GOAL 63

TAKE MASSIVE ACTION TOWARDS THE GOAL 66

LAW OF INERTIA 66
TAKE MASSIVE DIRECTED ACTION NOW 68
FOCUS ATTENTION 70
SET A DEADLINE 73

FAILURES AND PERSISTENCE 75

FAILURES ARE YOUR FRIENDS 75
LIFE'S PERSISTENCE TEST 77

FUEL FOR ACHIEVING GOALS 80

BURNING DESIRE TO ACHIEVE A GOAL 80
BIG WHAT 83
BIG WANT 86
BIG WHY 87
EMOTIONAL VISUALIZATION TEST 90
ENJOY WHAT YOU DO AS AN EXCITING GAME 92
MAKE ACHIEVING GOALS A GAME 93
SUCCESS BREEDS SUCCESS 94
SUCCESS LOG AND VIRTUAL SUPPORT GROUP 96
SUPPORT OF OTHER PEOPLE IN REACHING YOUR GOAL 98

LAST 5 MINUTES OF THE DAY 101

CELEBRATE SUCCESS AND REWARD YOURSELF 101

  DAILY PROGRESS AND DAILY PLAN 102

THE IDEA LIFESTYLE 105
  THINK AND REST 105
  EXPOSE YOURSELF TO NEW EXPERIENCES 108
  TRAIN CREATIVE MUSCLES 110

FINAL CHECKLIST 113

WHAT TO READ NEXT? 116

BIOGRAPHY 117

Introduction

Imagine that you have a magic Aladdin lamp and every time you rub it a genie appears and says, "I will fulfill any of your desires." Whether you say, "I want to become a millionaire," "I want to travel around the world," "I want to get married," or "I want to lose weight," the genie will fulfill your wish. How would your life change if you had such a lamp?

Of course magic lamps exist only in fairytales but you can become your own genie and fulfill your dreams whenever you want if you have a big enough desire and use an effective strategy. The Achievement Factory is an effective and easy-to-use system for fulfilling dreams no matter how big. It is based on many years of research of principles that high achievers use to generate excellent ideas, take massive action without procrastination and finish every day successfully. Thousands of Achievement Factory students have noticed that after implementation of this system, they achieve their dreams with almost 100% probability and their path towards achievements became several times shorter.

After you begin using the principles of the Achievement Factory, every day will bring you closer to fulfillment of your dreams, and this progress will breathe happiness and adventures into your life. I hope that what you learn in this book will change your life for the better as it changed the lives of thousands of people who use the Achievement Factory system daily to fulfill their dreams. Let's begin our journey.

Happiness

Happiness theory

I have met many people who were satisfied with their lives, but nobody as happy as Jason. In his 48 years, he has built a company that made him a multimillionaire, lived happily for 25 years with his wife, traveled around the world for 365 days, climbed Mt. Everest, won a national dancing competition and if I continue this list we will have enough material for several adventure novels. But what impressed me the most about Jason was the happiness that he radiates. When he speaks he is always smiling, he is passionate about life and genuinely interested in the person he talks to, and this energy of happiness is contagious. Once I asked, "Jason, what is the secret of your happiness?" and Jason replied:

"When you ask 'What is happiness?' the majority of people give a quite vague definition and as a result don't have a clear understanding of what, specifically, they can do today in order to increase the amount of happiness in their life. The secret of my happiness lies in a clear understanding of what happiness is. 'Happiness is the emotion of progress towards a desirable goal.' Numerous psychologists agree that working on your own goals and achieving small successes daily is what makes your life happy.

"Somebody wants to become a millionaire, somebody wants to travel around the world, somebody wants to get married, somebody wants to raise children, somebody wants to get a promotion at work, somebody wants to learn a foreign language and somebody wants to make a cozy interior in the house. For happiness the nature of your goal doesn't matter, what matters is that you really want to achieve it and that you regularly make progress.

"Sometimes you can hear from people who don't understand what happiness is: 'Be happy with what you already have.' This basically means: 'Don't ever be happy.' A human always wants more, this is our nature, and making progress towards desirable goals is a prerequisite for happiness. My rule of thumb, Jason's rule says: 'If you want to be happy, set a goal, give yourself what you want as quickly as possible and then set a new goal. Never suppress your dreams and desires.'

"Those people who never experience small victories fall into the opposite state of happiness called depression. Psychologists from the University of Liverpool have found that people with depression either don't have goals or their goals are so general that it is impossible to make regular progress towards achieving them. Of course there are unnatural sources of happiness such as drugs, alcohol, chocolate, extreme sports or smoking, however they give a very short-term feeling of happiness and for a cost of severely affecting health and long-term happiness.

"When young children play computer games they regularly make progress by getting from one level to another, by winning battles or gaining points. These accomplishments allow children to regularly experience a sense of satisfaction, accomplishment and victory. This concentrated emotion of progress leads to a release of endorphins in the brain and feeling of happiness. Computer games are a simulation of the happy life in the real world, and that's why they are so popular among kids. If you use the concept of regular achievements from computer games, you will become both a screenwriter and a hero of your life and will experience happy moments more often. I perceive my life as a 'computer game' and the reason for my happiness is the progress I make daily on the way to the goals I really want to achieve.

"Many people think they will become happy only after certain event in their life. They say: 'I will become happy once I win a million dollars in a lottery,' 'I will become happy once I win an Olympic gold medal,' 'I will become happy once I graduate from Harvard University' or 'I will be happy once I get married.' Unfortunately for them when this particular event happens the happiness doesn't last long, they quickly get used to what they already have and begin to want more. And it's normal, because everyone wants to be happy and the recipe for happiness is always getting more of what you want and don't have.

"Remember that you are happy not because of what you already have achieved but from the progress you make towards a desirable goal. Not your marital status, bank account or the size of a house give the feeling of happiness but PROGRESS. For example, a person who earns $1,000 per month is equally happy while making progress towards the goal of earning $2,000 per month as a person who earns $1M while making progress towards the goal of earning $2M. The fact that progress equals happiness can be explained by our brain's reward system which releases dopamine after we make measurable progress towards a goal in order to encourage our effort towards accumulating desirable achievements in our life.

"It's also critical to remember that happiness isn't just about making progress, but it's about making progress towards the desirable goal. If you are pursuing a goal that doesn't inspire you and isn't the one you truly want to achieve, then you will experience no joy from progress and accomplishment.

"Andrii, the greatest need of the human is a sense of purpose in life and making regular progress towards desirable goals gives you a sense of purpose. The reason I am happy is because I experience progress and celebrate success daily. Just like children are addicted to computer games I am addicted to life, because I am happy and it feels great."

Happiness comes to those who are moving toward something they want very much to happen. – Earl Nightingale

Look for a situation in which your work will give you as much happiness as your spare time. – Pablo Picasso

If you want to be happy, set a goal that commands your thoughts, liberates your energy, and inspires your hopes. – Andrew Carnegie, the richest man in America in the early 1900s

3 keys to an exciting life

Have you ever observed the excitement of young children when they open their Christmas presents? The experience of playing with wrapping paper and opening a present often brings them much more joy than a present itself. Both for children and adults, experiences impact their happiness much more than physical possessions. Although buying a new toy, a watch or a car brings short-term satisfaction, experiences bring satisfaction that lasts far longer. Many people who have a lot of money are unhappy, however those people who have a lot of positive experiences are always happy. Gather your own fortune of experiences, because experiences are more valuable than gold and make life happy. Over the course of my life I have met hundreds of people who live lives full of adventures and asked them, "What recommendation can you give to a person who wants to make his or her life more exciting?" Although these people were very different they told me very similar things, and their recommendations can be summarized in just 3 points.

Firstly, live your life as an adventure story. You are both a writer and a main character of the book describing the story of your life, and if the plot is interesting you will be excited to wake up every morning and take part in adventures. Deliberately fill your life with chapter after chapter of amazing life experiences and magical moments that fascinate you. Live your life so that when you grow old and tell a story of your life to your great-grandchildren, they will listen in awe and then say to their friends at school, "My great-grandfather (or great-grandmother) is cool!" Live your life as an adventure story and you will have an exciting life.

Secondly, live your life as a competition. Raise your standards and aim for continual progress in important areas of your life. No matter in which area of life you want to become better, today you compete with yesterday's you and tomorrow you will compete with today's you. If you win in this competition regularly you will notice progress, you will admire yourself and experience plenty of happy moments. Everybody who is doing well today in any area of life was once doing poorly and got to where he or she is today by making small wins regularly. If you live your life as a competition and become a little bit better every day you will fulfill all your dreams and have an exciting life.

Finally, live your life as an exploration. Explore the world by doing what you have never done before, by visiting places you have never been to before, by meeting people you haven't known before. The biggest breakthroughs in life happen when you expand your comfort zone and explore the world beyond the border of what you are familiar with. Often people are afraid of going outside of their comfort zone, however in 99% of cases what they fear isn't dangerous at all. Ask yourself: "What do I fear to do, but will bring me joy if I do it?" Live your life as an exploration, expand your comfort zone, experiment and you will have an exciting life.

Everyone, once in a while, asks himself or herself: "How can I make my life more exciting?" This question is extremely important because answers that you come to may impact one of the most important things in life – your happiness. Nobody can answer this question besides you but I hope that these 3 recommendations from people who already found their answers for themselves will help you to come up with valuable ideas.

Life isn't about finding yourself. Life is about creating yourself. – George Bernard Shaw

The person who has lived the most is not the one with the most years but the one with the richest experiences. – Jean-Jacques Rousseau

Twenty years from now you will be more disappointed by the things that you didn't do than by the ones you did do so throw off the bowlines. Sail away from the safe harbor. Catch the trade winds in your sails. Explore. Dream. Discover. – Mark Twain

Your life is in your hands

Self-responsibility for your life

Imagine that you are listening to a speaker in a room where the temperature is extremely low. All the people in the audience are freezing, however don't do anything about it. They just complain. Somebody says: "Oh, I am freezing!" And somebody answers, "Everybody is freezing. Not only you." Somebody says, "I didn't choose this room for the conference. It's the organizer's fault." And somebody answers, "Today is just an unlucky day for all of us." Finally a speaker says, "It's all winter's fault! If there was no winter it wouldn't be cold in the room."

You may think: "It doesn't make sense to suffer the cold for no reason. Most people would wear a jacket, drink hot coffee, do physical exercises, leave the room or ask a speaker to turn on the heating. Of course people would do at least something to eliminate the discomfort."

You are absolutely right. Of course most people understand that they can't control external circumstances such as the weather. The only thing they can do is react to them by taking certain action. If you are cold you would rather wear a jacket, a hat and gloves than just complain about the weather.

When you don't have what you want or what you dream about, you feel discomfort. Isn't this situation similar to the cold audience? You might say, "I don't have what I want because my manager doesn't value me, because the economy is bad, because competition is tough, because I am too old, because I am too young, because my partner deceived me, because my parents weren't rich or because I was born in the wrong country." You know what is the saddest? The saddest is that you will find many people saying, "Yes, life is tough. Yes, all these circumstances are the reasons you don't have what you want. Put up with the fact that you will never live the life of your dreams."

The truth is that no one can control external circumstances. No one can control age, the economy, the competition, the weather or the behavior of other people. The only thing you can control is your actions. No matter how bad the circumstances are it is always possible to get what you want; however, to get it you need to believe in the statement: "I am 100% responsible for everything that happens in my life. My actions, not the circumstances, create my future."

There are people who without legs win running competitions. There are people who without higher education become scientists. There are people who without starting capital create successful businesses. However, there are no people who get what they want by making excuses and blaming the circumstances.

People who are successful always talk about what they want and what they will do to achieve it. People who aren't talk about circumstances that don't let them live the life they want. Your life is in your hands only and the only person who can make it either miserable or exceptional is YOU. Whether you succeed or fail say to yourself: "I am 100% responsible for everything that happens in my life. My actions, not the circumstances, create my future." If you truly believe in this statement you are already on the highway towards the life of your dreams.

Ninety-nine percent of all failures come from people who have a habit of making excuses. — George Washington Carver, botanist who discovered over 325 uses for the peanut

You must take personal responsibility. You cannot change the circumstances, the seasons, or the wind, but you can change yourself. — Jim Rohn, America's foremost business philosopher

Believe that you can and will achieve a goal

For thousands of years after the first Olympic Games in ancient Greece it was firmly believed that running a mile in under 4 minutes was not only impossible, but also dangerous. Doctors and scientists claimed, "Even if a human ever runs a sub-four minute mile his or her heart would explode." Imagine, how hard you would push yourself in training and competitions as a runner, if you shared the belief that your heart could explode?

Then in the 1950s, in England, a medical student named Roger Bannister, as part of his medical research, studied anatomy and physiology of the human body and looked for medical evidence of a physical limitation to run a sub-four minute mile. Roger came to the conclusion that not only will the heart not explode, but also that a human is more than capable of running the mile in less than 4 minutes. He was so confident in his findings that he announced to the world, "I personally will break the record and prove that running a 4-minute mile is possible!"

The Achievement Factory

On May 6, 1954, in Oxford, Roger Bannister made his mark in history. He broke the world record and ran a mile in 3 minutes and 59.4 seconds. Unbelievably, just 46 days later a runner from Australia ran a mile in 3 minutes and 58.0 seconds, and within the next 5 years 20 more runners ran a mile in less than 4 minutes. What had been considered impossible for thousands of years was accomplished by 20 people within 5 years after they changed their belief.

Some people think, "I doubt that I can achieve my goal." As a result, this doubt prevents their subconscious minds from generating ideas, keeps them from pushing themselves hard enough and eventually they give up after meeting a first obstacle and say: "I was right when I said that I couldn't achieve my goal." If you believe that you are limited in intelligence, creativity or talent, you will act as if you are indeed limited in that particular area. The biggest reason why people fail is not their lack of abilities but their lack of belief in their abilities. No matter what you believe in, your brain will look for confirmations that you are right and will eventually find them. As Henry Ford said, "Whether you think you can, or you think you can't – you're right."

History has numerous examples of when people, even in the most unfavorable circumstances, achieved their goals: poor people became rich, people with bad health became athletes and people who were considered mentally retarded became scientists. If you say, "I have 100% confidence that I will achieve my goal," you will find a solution, you will take massive action, you will overcome any obstacles and after achieving a goal will say, "I was right when I said that I can achieve my goal!"

The magical invocation that successful people use to achieve their goals is "I can." On the way to your goal tell yourself "I can" every day, and if anybody ever says "You can't" say "I can." You can achieve literally whatever you want if you have a big enough desire and belief that you can.

If you want to be successful, it's just this simple. Know what you are doing. Love what you are doing. And believe in what you are doing. – Will Rogers

The only thing that stands between a man and what he wants from life is often merely the will to try it and the faith to believe that it is possible. – Richard M. DeVos

The future belongs to those who believe in the beauty of their dreams. – Eleanor Roosevelt

Commitment to achieve a goal

In 331 BC, with an army of 35,000 men, Alexander the Great arrived at the shores of Persia to fight with Persian king Darius III. Upon arriving, soldiers from Alexander's army realized that they were greatly outnumbered by the 200,000-member army of the enemy. They pleaded to their young leader: "Alexander, we should delay the attack. Let's go back home to return later with more men." As the legend says, Alexander ordered his soldiers to burn their boats and said: "We go home in Persian ships, or we die!" Alexander's soldiers realized that the only way to survive was to win. They committed to return home alive and in one of the most dramatic battles of all times defeated the Persians.

There is a significant difference between, "I wish to achieve my goal" and "I am committed to achieve my goal." If you wish to achieve your goal it means, "I will accept it if it falls into my lap." You will do what is easy and convenient on the way to the goal, but once faced with difficulties you will find excuses and give up. However, if you decide to be committed, it means, "I will achieve my goal no matter what. Failure is not an option." Commitment is when you have burned the ships and there is no room for a backup in your mind.

Since I graduated high school, my dream was to pass the Cisco Certified Internetwork Expert certification (CCIE), which even today is considered the most prestigious and difficult IT certification to obtain in the world. This certification is considered so difficult not only because of the enormous amount of information you need to know but also because of the extremely difficult lab part of the exam where you need to configure a network of 10 devices according to the suggested scenario within 8 hours. After 3 years of intensive preparation and one day before I was supposed to fly to Brussels to take my chance in the lab part of the exam, my mother asked: "What if you don't pass the exam in the first attempt? What is your plan B?"

I said, "Mom, I will definitely pass! Since I don't have a full-time job like the majority of engineers who attempt to pass CCIE, I won't have enough money to finance the second attempt. I will also not have enough time to prepare for the second attempt. I have been practicing for 16 hours a day for 4 months in the last phase of my preparation. I didn't attend classes at the university the entire months of September and October and have received a notification that I might be expelled. I don't have any other option rather than to pass now. I don't have a plan B." After I passed the exam I looked back at everything I did including the possible and the impossible on the way to my dream and realized: "My burning desire to earn a CCIE and a 100% commitment were the reasons for my success. If, again, I have such a burning desire and commitment to achieve another dream, nothing will be able to stop me."

Having a plan B is dangerous, because if you have it you won't do 100% of what you can to implement your plan A. You may stop trying to achieve a goal after the first few failures and eventually end up with this plan B. When you are committed, you give your mind an order to think about solutions and give yourself no space to think about excuses. The secret of incredible commitment is simple: "Determine which dream could have the biggest positive impact on your happiness. Make a promise to yourself to fulfill this dream no matter how difficult it is."

Create a dream list

Allow yourself to dream and have a desire

Imagine that you are 90 years old. You sit comfortably in an armchair and around you sit all your children, grandchildren and great-grandchildren. They say, "Granny, Granny! (Or Grandpa, Grandpa!) You lived such a fascinating life. Your life is one of the greatest adventures that we have ever heard about. Everything you ever dreamed about came true. Please, tell us one more time how it all began."

You smile and begin your story, "Well, many years ago I found an ancient Aladdin lamp. When I rubbed it a genie appeared and said, 'This is a magic lamp and I am an almighty genie. I will fulfill everything you ask me for. And I can fulfill not 3, not 5 but an unlimited number of your desires. The only thing I can't do is to decide what you truly want.'

"I said, 'That's amazing, genie. I will certainly ask you for many things to turn my life into the life of my dreams. I didn't ever expect to meet you and don't have a list of my desires ready for you. Can I take an hour to clarify what I want and write down all my desires?'

"And the genie said, 'Sure. And to help you clarify all your desires I will share with you a "100 dreams exercise." This exercise is extremely effective and will help you to identify everything you want at this point. Once you complete this exercise and clearly know your desires, we will be already halfway towards making your life an adventure. The dream that you don't know you have will never get fulfilled, that's why the time you spend thinking about your desires is perhaps the most effectively spent time in your life."

100 dreams exercise

Write down all your dreams

Your task is to write down a minimum of 100 desires that you would ask a genie to fulfill if you had a magic lamp. This could be literally anything: small desires, big desires, physical possessions, relationships, achievements or experiences. Imagine what your perfect life would look like and think about which desires would bring you from where you are to the life in your imagination. Spend at least 1 hour thinking about what you would want if there were no limitations and you could get and achieve anything. Don't worry about making this list perfect, as you will be able to change or update it in the future. The most important thing in this exercise is the quantity of desires, which should be not less than 100.

You will probably write the first 20 desires really quickly because they are at the top of your mind. Once you exhaust desires you have thought about before, your subconscious will begin really thinking. Desires that are between numbers 60 and 100 are usually the most original desires that you haven't considered before.

According to research done by Dominican University, people who just think about their goals achieve them with 43% probability. People who not only think about their goals but also write down their goals achieve them with 61%

probability. Finally, people who write down their goals, create action plans and check progress weekly increase their chances for success to 76%. Isn't that impressive that just by thinking about what you want you can achieve your goal with 43% probability and writing down your goal increases this probability by another 20%? Later in the book you will learn principles that will allow you to raise this probability to 100%, however at this point you need to understand that clearly knowing what you want and putting it on paper is perhaps the most important step towards the life of your dreams.

This exercise is extremely important to make your life more exciting as it allows you to realize what you want, and realizing what you want is already at least 50% of success. Thousands of successful people around the world achieved their dreams using principles from this book and I promise that you will achieve anything you truly want if you use the same principles. You will become your own genie.

3 magic questions for identifying desires

Did you write all 100 desires in the previous exercise? The more desires you write down, the more you clarify for yourself what could make your life more exciting. The following 3 questions are my favorites because they are extremely effective for generating ideas for your life desires list.

1) How would you live your life if you had a billion dollars?

People often limit their desires by thinking about their current salary, savings or job. Thinking about this question will allow you to identify what you would do, have or be if money wasn't a problem. To live the life of your dreams, you first need to understand how the life of your dreams looks.

Once you identify clearly what you really dream about, you will be able to develop a plan for fulfilling a dream no matter what your current circumstances are.

2) If you were guaranteed success, what would you do?

People often limit their desires by thinking about potential failures and obstacles. This question will allow you to decide which desires would make your life more fulfilling if you were guaranteed success. The answers to this question are certainly great candidates for your 100 dreams list and once fulfilled will make your life an exciting adventure.

3) Remember all the moments in your life when you felt alive, excited and happy. How could you bring more such moments to your life?

You have experienced a lot of happy moments in the past that psychologist Abraham Maslow has identified as "peak experiences." One of your aims in life is to enjoy as many happy moments as possible. If you clearly understand what caused these happy moments in the past, you will have ideas for desires that need to be added to your dreams list in order to experience more of these peak experiences in the future.

I have tested numerous questions in identifying the true desires of my students, and these 3 questions proved to be the most effective for many years. Ask yourself these questions to come up with great ideas for your dreams.

Four areas of goals setting

There are 4 major areas of life that you need to develop in order to live a happy and fulfilling life: body and health, career and business, socialization and family, and personal development.

1) Body and health

The healthy body is the vehicle that can get you to a happy and fulfilling life. The desires from this area are related to improvement of your health or body. For example: "I want to become more energetic after losing 20 pounds," "I want to become more flexible by attending yoga for 3 months," "I want to gain more control over my body by learning how to dance salsa," "I want to become more energetic by developing a habit of stretching every morning," "I want to be able to do 25 pull-ups" or "I want to make my daily diet more healthy by excluding certain foods."

2) Career and business

The career and business section covers your financial goals, the way you want to earn money, to self-realize and to contribute to society. Are you doing what you love each day to earn money? Do you have enough money to live the life of your dreams? What do you want to achieve that will make you proud and self-fulfilled? Desires from this section will help you to earn more money, to have fun doing it and to feel that what you do has a purpose and meaning.

3) Socialization and family

Social desires are targeted at improving your relationships with family or your interactions with friends or strangers. For example, "Take family on vacation to Hawaii," "Take parents to the restaurant," "Meet 20 new people in the city I am moving to," "Attend a conference and start a conversation with at least 10 strangers," or "Sign up for dance classes together with a friend." Social goals are just anything that will allow you to either meet new people or to maintain relationships with people who you already know.

4) Personal development

Personal development desires are any desires that will enrich you intellectually or spiritually. For example: "I want to travel through Europe for one month," "I want to write a novel," "I want to read at least 20 nonfiction books within a year," "I want to learn a new skill" or " I want to overcome a fear of public speaking." Being in a constant state of personal development keeps you growing.

Depending on your preferences and time in your life, you may dedicate more time to reaching desires in one area than in the other 3, however you can't completely ignore any of these 4 areas. If you devote all your efforts to developing your career, you may feel unhappy if you have family problems or don't have a family. If you have an amazing family, you may feel unhappy because you have poor health and little energy. If you have great income, an excellent family and excellent health, you may not feel completely happy if you are not pursuing any desires in the personal development area.

You can have more desires in areas that you are most interested in, however remember that you need to have at least some desires in each of the areas in order to have a happy and fulfilling life. These 4 areas also greatly support each other. For example, if you have great social connections and a happy family life, you will be more successful in your work. If you have excellent health, you will have a better mood and will have better family relationships. If you invest time in personal development, you might be more successful in your work and at building social connections.

Now return to the 100 dreams exercise and write down more desires in areas that you haven't covered thoroughly yet. Being in the constant flow of setting and achieving goals in each of the 4 life areas is a key to a happy, adventurous and successful life.

Creating dreams is a continuous process

After you have completed the 100 dreams exercise and written down on paper all the dreams you could come up with, you need to think periodically about what else you may want and add new dreams to this list. Remember that an exceptional life consists of two parts: coming up with new desires, and making them a reality. If you want to make your life an adventure, you need to understand that dreaming and coming up with new desires is a continuous process.

Make it a habit to spend at least 15 minutes every 2 weeks thinking about "What else would I want if everything were possible or what else could I ask for if I had a magic wand?" You will realize that during each of these sessions new ideas will come to your mind.

Firstly, when you think about what you want regularly, you activate your subconscious mind and it thinks about your desires 24/7. If you think about what you want twice a month for 15 minutes it doesn't mean that your subconscious thinks about your desires for 30 minutes in total, it means it thinks about them 30 days round the clock. Thinking regularly about desires for short periods of time will give you far more ideas than a single super-long creative session.

Secondly, your life experiences are raw materials and inspiration for new ideas, which are essentially combinations of old ideas. As you live your life, fulfill desires and experience different events your subconscious gains more data for creativity and will be able to create excellent fresh ideas for desires that it wasn't able to create before.

Happiness is a process of setting goals and achieving them, however to achieve goals you first need to clearly understand what you want. Even the most experienced shooter can't hit the target if he or she doesn't see it. Every time you absolutely clearly understand what your desire is, you are already halfway towards making it happen.

Every once in a while think about your desires and add ideas to your dream list. Remember that in order to live the life of your dreams you first need to clearly understand how exactly the life of your dreams looks. Ask yourself, "What do I want?" and listen to what your inner voice says. This conversation needs to take place regularly to keep your dreams list up to date with goals that are most desirable at the current stage of your life. Creating and fulfilling desires is a continuous process.

Don't limit yourself. Many people limit themselves to what they think they can do. You can go as far as your mind lets you. – Mary Kay Ash

Realize what you really want. It stops you from chasing butterflies and puts you to work digging gold. – William Moulton Marsden

The indispensable first step to getting the things you want out of life is this: decide what you want. – Ben Stein, actor and author

Prioritization

Prioritize goals and be ready to pay the price

When I was 7, at the school where I studied, there was a casting call for the boys' choir. I enjoyed singing so after classes I went to the school cafeteria and asked a lady who was sitting at the piano, "How can I participate in the casting?" She hit a key on the piano and asked me to sing the note "Do." I tried my best to repeat the sound, but could see that the lady didn't like how I sang. She hit another key on the piano and asked me to repeat the note "Re." I tried my best but could see that she again didn't like what I did. After several more attempts she said, "You have no ear for music. Unfortunately, I can't recommend you to the choir." At the age of 21, when I was a highly paid IT engineer, I recalled my childhood desire to sing and thought, "In my childhood I couldn't study in the free school choir because I didn't pass the casting. Today, I can afford a private singing coach and he or she will teach me whether I have an ear for music or not."

After my first class with one of the best private singing coaches in the city, she asked: "Andrii, how much do you want to sing? You see, because of your natural ear for music you will make progress much slower than my other students. You will never be able to become a great singer but probably after 1,000 hours of practice you will be able to sing in a circle of friends. Please think and let me know if you are ready to pay this price for your goal."

At home the following conversation took place in my head: "I am very purposeful and if I decide to achieve a goal of becoming a better singer I will achieve it no matter what. But is this my first-priority goal? No. I want to become a better dancer, learn German and develop my business more than I want to become a better singer and if I invest 1,000 hours in one of these goals right now I would be happier. Is becoming a better singer worth its price for me? No, 1,000 hours is too expensive for the goal of being able to sing in a circle of friends. What should I do to become happier? I should focus on goals I want to achieve the most and on the goals that I am ready to pay for with the necessary amount of time, money and willpower."

Imagine that you enter a goals supermarket and see a price tag next to each goal you have to pay for with your time and resources: To be able to do 100 pull-ups – 200 hours of training on the bar. Become an Olympic Games gold medal winner – 6 years of training, 4 hours per day at least 310 days a year. Become a world famous violin player – 10,000 hours of practice. Become a multimillionaire – 20 years of intense work without weekends, thousands of failures, rejections and disappointments. Travel around the world – 6 months of time and $30,000.

Your wallet has a limited amount of hours and resources. Even if you are extremely purposeful and wealthy you can't buy everything in the goals supermarket and need to prioritize your "purchases." For example, if you decide to become an Olympic Games gold medal winner, a world-famous writer and travel around the world, you can't achieve all these goals simultaneously because the number of hours in a day is limited; however, you can achieve them sequentially. Ask yourself, "What one goal is most important for me, and the achieving of which would have the biggest positive impact on my life?" According to research you can effectively work without losing focus only on several major goals simultaneously. Pick your one or two major goals and start pursuing them right now; leave all others for the future.

For each of the goals, you need to determine a price in terms of time and resources and decide if you are ready to pay it or not. For example, everyone may want to become a multimillionaire, but not everyone is ready to pay the price for it that consists of time, disappointments and deprivation of daily pleasures. For most people who want to improve their financial situation, a goal of earning a six-figure salary may be more reasonable in terms of the price they have to pay. Everyone wants to become an Olympic Games gold medal winner but not everyone is ready for the price it costs in terms of hours of training. For most people, a goal of being able to do 100 pull-ups or run a marathon may be more reasonable. Everybody would like to be a world-famous writer, but not everyone is ready to spend 10,000 hours on writing. For most people, writing just one book may be much more compelling.

Once you have created a list of your dreams, prioritize them and determine how much each of them may cost you in terms of time and resources. Choose your highest-priority desires and for each of them ask yourself, "Am I truly committed to pay the price to achieve this goal?" If the answer is yes, begin working towards this goal; there is virtually nothing that can stop you. If you are truly passionate about your goal, paying the price by accomplishing the necessary amount of work to achieve it will be much more pleasurable because you will enjoy the process rather than suffer through it.

If people knew how hard I had to work to gain my mastery, it wouldn't seem wonderful at all. – Michelangelo (Renaissance sculptor and painter, who spent 4 years lying on his back painting the ceiling of the Sistine Chapel)

3 super-productivity questions

If you want to fulfill your desire as soon as possible, you need to increase your productivity. The experience of thousands of successful people shows that if you regularly ask yourself the 3 super-productivity questions below, you will be able to significantly optimize the use of your time.

Occasionally ask yourself the first super-productivity question, "Is this particular action I am doing right now getting me closer to my goal or further away?" There are no neutral actions. Everything you do either gets you closer to the goal or postpones achieving the destination. A study by Vouchercloud.com found that office workers on average are productive only 2 hours and 53 minutes per day. The rest of the time is spent on distractions such as checking social networks, reading news websites or discussing out-of-work activities with colleagues. If after asking this question you switch, at least sometimes, from a distracting activity to an activity that gets you closer to the goal, your productivity will increase.

Ask yourself a second super-performance question, "What is the most valuable use of my time right now?" According to

Pareto principles, 20% of activities bring 80% of results. Make sure that after asking this question you work on the task that makes the biggest progress in the direction of the goal.

A third super-productivity question is, "How can I do what I am doing more effectively?" If you come up with ideas of how to optimize the process you use, how to cut unnecessary steps from the work you do or how to delegate simple tasks, you will manage to do more in less time.

Asking super-productivity questions will allow you to make sure that your actions get you closer to the goal, that your actions produce the biggest result and that your processes are optimized. The more effectively you use your time, the quicker you will achieve your goal and the sooner you will live the life of your dreams.

The things that matter most must never be at the mercy of the things that matter least. – Goethe

How to set goals

Ask any successful person, "How did you get to where you are in life?" He or she will most probably say, "By setting and achieving goals." Once you have decided to fulfill your dream, formulate it as a specific, measurable and achievable goal. Goals serve as a GPS navigator that sets a direction and lets you know whether a particular action or idea takes you closer to the destination or further away. Setting a goal effectively has the biggest impact on whether you achieve what you want or not, because in order to get to the destination you first need to know what this destination is. The most powerful goals are those that are measurable, specific and achievable because they set clearly a direction that needs to be followed in order to achieve them. To shorten a path towards the life of your dreams, make sure that you always set goals that are specific, measurable and achievable.

Specific and measurable goal

Imagine that you have a little genie inside you who can fulfill any of your desires. Whatever you ask the genie for, he will fulfill. However, ask cautiously because this genie is naughty and will fulfill the desires exactly as you formulate them. If there is a way to fulfill your desire and leave you unhappy, be sure the genie will fulfill it this way. For example, you say, "Genie, I want a BIG change in my life." Next year you may have a divorce and this will be a BIG change in your life, just as you asked. If you say, "I want a car," you will get a 20-year-old car. If you say, "I want to significantly lose weight," you will have severe diarrhea.

Imagine that you live in New York, wake up in the morning and decide, "I want to go to the Empire State Building." Whether you decide to go there by car, by subway or by walking you will definitely get there. Why? Firstly, because the address of the Empire State Building is very specifically defined and you will be able to choose the direction of movement properly. Secondly, because you will be able to track your progress and see that with time you are getting closer to the destination. And finally, you will clearly understand whether you already reached your destination or not.

Setting a goal is very similar to getting from point A to point B in the city. If you know very clearly what your goal is, you will always reach the destination because you know its address. Desires are often fulfilled just as if a naughty genie was fulfilling them. The more clearly you formulate your goal, the more likely you will get what you want in a way you want and experience joy after getting it.

Instead of formulating a goal like "I want more money," say "I want to save $50,000." Instead of saying "I want to be fit," say "I want to be able to do 100 pushups." Instead of saying "I want to travel around the world," say "I want to spend a week in Rome." Fifty thousand dollars, 100 pushups and a week in Rome are specific enough goals for you to develop a plan on how to achieve them, to see if your effort got you closer to them and if you already reached them.

Many people make a lot of chaotic movements in their life without having clear goals and then wonder why they don't live the lives of their dreams. People who do indeed live the lives of their dreams always spend enough time to clarify their goals before moving anywhere. No matter how fast they are capable of moving, they always get what they want because every single step brings them closer to the destination.

There is a direct relationship between everything you achieve in life and how clearly you specify your goals, because clarity of your goals impacts the preciseness and effectiveness of your actions. That's why the most important step towards living the life of your dreams is to define as specifically as possible what exactly you want. So specifically that a 7-year-old child could explain what your goal is and determine whether you achieved it or not. It's impossible to hit a target that you can't see, that's why before taking any actions you should ask yourself, "Did I define my goal specifically enough?" and if the answer is yes, think about how you can make it even more specific.

In the absence of clearly-defined goals, we become strangely loyal to performing daily trivia until ultimately we become enslaved by it. – Robert A. Heinlein

If you really know what you want out of life, it's amazing how opportunities will come to enable you to carry them out. – John Goddard, great life adventurer

Everyone wants to improve their life. We can have these big ambitions, but if we don't break those down and set specific goals, we're not ever going to get anywhere. – Crystal Paine

Set achievable goals

When you formulate a goal make sure that the goal is within your control. The only thing you can control in life is you and your actions. Set the goals that depend only on you, not luck, circumstances or other people. For example, if you set a goal "Win a dancing competition," this goal doesn't depend fully on you, it also depends on your competitors and the judges. However if you set a goal "Practice dancing for 200 hours under supervision of a world-famous instructor and 500 hours on my own," this goal is completely under your control.

Also make sure that the goal is theoretically achievable or otherwise you will fail with a 100% guarantee. What is a theoretically unachievable goal then? For example, to earn a million dollars is an achievable goal. But to earn a million dollars next month is a theoretically unachievable goal if your income this month was $1,000 and you don't have a breakthrough idea of how to increase it quickly by 1,000 times. To run a mile in 3 minutes 43 seconds is an achievable goal. But to run a mile in 5 seconds is a theoretically unachievable goal due to limitations of the human body. To learn 10,000 foreign words is an achievable goal. But to learn 10,000 foreign words within 1 day is an unachievable goal if you don't have superpowers.

Sometimes, people set goals they have little control over, or that are theoretically unachievable, and then get disappointed after failure. The worst thing that can happen after failure is that you may lose faith in goal setting, say "Goal setting doesn't work" and stop moving towards making your life exceptional. Set goals that stretch you, but make sure that they are completely under your control and are theoretically achievable. If you do, you will have more motivation to take action towards your goals and as a result will achieve them more often.

A good goal is like a strenuous exercise – it makes you stretch. – Mary Kay Ash

Most people overestimate what they can do in one year and underestimate what they can do in ten years. – Bill Gates

Without goals and plans to reach them, you are like a ship that has set sail with no destination. – Fitzhugh Dodson

3 timeframes for goals

Create a compelling vision

In his research, Dr. Edward Banfield, a Harvard psychologist, wanted to discover why some people become financially independent in the course of their lives and others don't. At the beginning of the research he expected that the answer would lie among such factors as intelligence, education, family background or relationships. However, Dr. Banfield discovered that the single factor that determined success was how far a person projects into the future while taking actions today.

The least successful members of society such as alcoholics or drug addicts have the lowest time perspective. They are focused on short-term pleasures and make decisions about their actions taking into account only how their life might look like in several hours. People who don't reach financial independence make decisions today considering only how their life will look like in a week, a month or a quarter. Successful people have a clear understanding of how they want their future to look in several years and make their decisions today based on this long-term vision. Dr. Banfield discovered that the further you think into the future, the better you make decisions today to make sure that this future becomes a reality and the more successful you become as a result.

Take time to dream and decide what your perfect life would look like in 5 years if everything were possible. Your 5-year vision should be so compelling that simply thinking about it will make you feel goose bumps and put a smile on your face. A clear and exciting vision will stimulate you to take actions today necessary to make it a reality in the future. The lives of happy and successful people are very different: some of them become Olympic Games winners, some build big corporations, some travel around the world, some become fluent in several languages and some become great parents; however, one thing that is common among them is that they all have a clear and compelling vision.

Creating or clarifying a vision is a process that can take you a day, a week or a month, however it is absolutely worth your time and can have an enormous positive impact on your life. If you have decided on a direction for your life, all your actions will move you further in that direction. If you haven't, some of your actions will move you forward, some backwards, some left, some right and eventually you might stay in one place. Knowing clearly how your dream life looks is the most important step towards making your dream life a reality.

Process goals

Besides a compelling vision for the next 1 to 10 years, you should also have a goal for the next 1 to 3 months to get closer to the life of your dreams. If a vision gives a general direction for your life, a process goal is a dream or a part of the dream to accomplish for which you are taking specific actions today. You might ask: "Why do you recommend setting goals for 1- 3 months?"

If you set a goal for one year, it's too far off and you may be enticed to procrastinate. A day is a very short period of time compared to a year, and you might think, "If I do nothing today, it won't be a big problem for meeting a deadline." If however you set a goal for a week, this time frame is too short for you to sense a tangible progress at the end and experience significant satisfaction from the result. That's why a perfect time frame for the goal is 1 to 3 months in order for you to feel that the deadline is close, and that every day matters from one side and to be motivated to take action because the result you can achieve is significant from the other.

For example, if you decide to win a national swimming competition in a year, you might think "Missing just one training won't be a big deal because I will have plenty of time to make it up." If however you set a goal for a week, you will barely be motivated imagining how great a swimmer you will be by achieving it. No matter how intensively you train, a week is a very short period of time to sense significant progress at the end. That's why setting a goal for 1 to 3 months will make you most productive in making your dreams a reality because it will stimulate you to take actions without procrastination and motivate by a compelling possible result.

You might reasonably ask, "But, Andrii, what if my dream takes longer than 3 months to fulfill. What should I do?" If your dream takes longer than 3 months to fulfill, split achieving it into blocks of 3 months because this period of time will make you the most productive and motivated. For example, imagine that you currently earn $1,000 per month and your dream, in a year, is to earn $5,000 per month. Split this goal into 4 sub goals: To earn $1,500 per month in 3 months, to earn $2,250 in 6 months, to earn $3,375 in 9 months and finally $5,000 in 12 months. If you split your goal into blocks of 3 months, you will feel more pressure to take action without procrastination, you will have higher motivation as you will regularly experience intermediate success and as a result you will be much more likely to achieve a goal on time.

The dream life consists of fulfilled dreams and each dream consists of one or more goals. The perfect time frame for the goal is 1 to 3 months. Decide what your goals are for the next 1- to 3-month block and begin pursuing them today.

Set a task for a day

In order to achieve a goal, you need to set a task for the day so that you clearly understand what to do each hour and have motivation to act. For example, if you prepare for swimming competitions, your daily task may be to swim a certain distance. If you create a title for your company, your daily task may be to generate a certain amount of ideas. If you prepare for an exam, your daily task may be to read a certain amount of book pages.

Many people make the mistake of setting long-term goals, however don't split them into clear and measurable daily tasks. As a result, they either feel overwhelmed and don't take actions towards the goal or after months of taking chaotic actions realize that their effort didn't bring the desired results. Split a goal into measurable daily tasks and by accomplishing each of them, you will make small but regular progress towards the destination. Each task you set for the day converts into specific actions that are feasible to accomplish and completely under your control.

People often become depressed and unmotivated if they work towards their goals for months and don't experience intermediate success. The key to maintaining motivation is setting tasks for each day, accomplishing them and celebrating the success. Sometimes the success you achieve will be small, sometimes big, but most important is that you experience joy from accomplishment every single day. If you know that, "In the evening I will recognize and celebrate everything I have accomplished during the day. It will feel great!" this thought will keep you motivated to act right now without procrastination.

Your success in life depends on how much you achieve within a year, the success within a year depends on how much you achieve within a month and your success within a month depends how much you achieve within a day. The task for today converts an abstract goal into specific actions that are within your control as well as motivates you to take them and make progress. As a result, you will be able to finish your day successfully, achieve your goals and eventually make your vision a reality.

When you chop a tree, the strength of your whacks is important but not as important as that they are all directed at the same spot. If they are, the strength of each whack will be accumulated and the tree will eventually fall; otherwise you will spend hours hitting chaotically without any result. The same is true for achieving your dreams. Productivity of your work is important but not as important as that all your actions are taken in the same direction. To maximize the accumulated effect from everything you do, always keep in mind your long-term vision, 1-3 months goal and the task for the day.

The secret of getting ahead is getting started. The secret of getting started is breaking your complex, overwhelming tasks into small manageable tasks, and then starting on the first one. — Mark Twain, celebrated American author and humorist

In essence, if we want to direct our lives, we must take control of our consistent actions. It's not what we do once in a while that shapes our lives, but what we do consistently. — Anthony Robbins

Visualization

What is visualization?

Memories are the replaying of past events in your head and visualization is the replaying of future events in your head. Imagine an event that happened to you last year, last month or yesterday in detail as clearly as possible. Now imagine what you really want to happen to you in the future in detail as clearly as possible. It may be a trip to a foreign country, a purchase of a new house or a big deal in business. Notice that the image quality in your head is the same for the future as for the past, although you were physically present in the past and saw everything with your own eyes, but you have never been in the future. Why does this happen?

When you visualize the future your optic nerve is directly involved and acts as if you were physically seeing what you are imagining. Your brain doesn't see the difference between reality and imagination and believes that what you visualize is indeed happening. When you regularly visualize the goal as already achieved, it creates a conflict in your subconscious mind between what you currently have and what you imagine. As a result, the subconscious does everything possible to resolve this conflict and to turn imaginary pictures into reality. Successful people know the power of visualization and regularly use it as a magic wand to turn their dreams into reality. You might ask, "Why is visualization that powerful?" About that in the next section…

Benefits of visualization

Visualization increases your desire to achieve a goal

Every time you visualize a moment when your goal is achieved you sense how pleasurable this moment will be and as a result increase your desire to achieve the goal. The higher your desire to achieve a goal, the more excited you are to wake up every morning and to take necessary actions in the direction of the goal. Visualizing the dream builds up your desire to make it a reality and this desire motivates you to take massive action without procrastination. If you regularly visualize a goal, your productivity increases and as a result you achieve a goal quicker than without visualization.

Visualization increases focus and directs actions

The rule of focus says: "What you focus your attention on is where your energy flows and what eventually gets done." Your thoughts control your body; the more you think about the goal, the more actions you make relevant to the goal and the faster you move towards achievement of the goal. As American Philosopher William James said, "Your physical actions are simply the outward manifestation of your inner thoughts. What you see in yourself is what you get out of yourself."

Every time you visualize your dream you focus your attention on this dream and simply by doing so increase the amount of actions you take and ideas you generate relevant to this dream. The more often you visualize your dream, the more you focus on this dream and the sooner it will be achieved. Visualization increases your focus and directs your thoughts and actions.

Visualization helps to activate the subconscious to generate ideas

When you work towards a goal, you constantly need ideas: "What actions should I take tomorrow?" "How do I fulfill this task?" "Where can I find the necessary resources?" The subconscious mind is responsible for generating ideas and if you give it a task, it will process thoughts during the day and during the night and eventually will give you solutions for any problem. When you visualize your goal, you give your subconscious a task: "Please create solutions that will help me to achieve my goal." If you don't think about your goal, the subconscious mind stays idle and does nothing. But if you occasionally visualize your goal, you activate your super-powerful subconscious mind to generate continuous flow of ideas and as a result the path towards the goal becomes clearer. The process of goal achievement consists of ideas and actions, and visualization positively influences both these components.

Visualization programs the brain's filter

Every second your brain receives about 10 million bits of information but allows into your awareness only those things that you consider important. Visualization programs your brain's filter to consider everything relevant to your goal as important. For example, if your goal is to become a world-class public speaker you will begin noticing books about public speaking in a library, advertisements of courses relevant to public speaking in magazines, and videos of great speakers on the internet. You might have seen all this information before, but because you didn't tell your brain's filter that this information is important, it was filtered out. If your brain is the radio, then visualization is a process of tuning the radio on a wave of your goal. After visualization, resources necessary for achieving a goal that you wouldn't notice otherwise will scream from everywhere, as the filter will mark them as worth the attention.

Imagine that your goal is to arrange a two-week family vacation. Firstly, you clearly visualize an ideal vacation in your head. Secondly, you gather information about different vacation options. Thirdly, you generate ideas about how to have the most fun during vacation at the lowest price. Finally, you buy tickets and pack a suitcase. Any achievement in life begins from the first mandatory step – visualization of the dream. Your mental picture serves as a GPS in your brain that directs your actions towards achievement of the goal. Once you have determined what you want, visualize your goal because visualization leads to ideas and enthusiasm, ideas and enthusiasm lead to actions, and actions lead to results. This is one of the most profound principles of success.

Imagination is everything. It is the preview of life's coming attractions. – Albert Einstein, winner, Nobel Prize for Physics

You must first visualize yourself as a success in order to be a success. – Rosa Diaz

If you can see it, and believe it, it is much easier to achieve it. – Oprah Winfrey

Visualization magic formula

Visualization of desire is perhaps the most powerful technique that successful people use to greatly accelerate achievement of their goals. If you tell your brain what you want often enough and clearly enough, it will turn any dream into reality. To achieve goals with 100% guarantee, visualize your ideal future taking into account the magic formula: clarity of visualization X regularity of visualization = achieved goal.

When visualizing a dream, think of a particular moment that sums up everything you associate with successful goal achievement. For example, it could be imagining yourself as the first runner crossing the finish line, imagining yourself receiving congratulations after a job promotion or imagining yourself driving the car of your dreams. Imagine yourself in the middle of the picture and experience a moment of goal achievement by all senses. Imagine what you see, what you hear and what you feel. Keep adding details until you can see a moment of goal achievement clearly. Visualization is perhaps the most powerful tool that successful people use, and its effectiveness directly depends on clarity of your mental picture in which you celebrate and enjoy the achievement of the goal. The more vividly you imagine a moment of goal achievement, the more real it becomes for your subconscious and the more effective visualization is for motivating actions, generating ideas and attracting resources. The more vividly you imagine fulfillment of your dream, the quicker it materializes in the real world.

Goals should be always at the top of your mind to keep the subconscious mind thinking about ideas, to maintain enthusiasm, and to notice necessary resources. The more frequently you visualize your goal as already achieved, the higher the overall impact of visualization on the process of goal achievement and the quicker the picture from your imagination will become reality.

An excellent way to increase the number of times you visualize a goal is to create a dream board. A dream board is a picture or a collection of images that represent what exactly you want to achieve. For example, it could be a picture of your dream car, it could be a picture of a check for $1 million, or a picture of a famous athlete with your head attached to his or her body. You can either draw a picture yourself or create a collage with pictures taken from magazines, newspapers or the internet. Hang your dream board near the desk where you work most of the time, so that you stumble upon it often during the day. The goal of the dream board is to remind you to visualize your goal every time you see it and increase the frequency of your visualizations. Every time you look at your dream board you will think, "Oh, here is my dream. Let's imagine this dream as already fulfilled in the future for a few seconds." With a dream board, you will think about your goal more often and as a result the overall impact of visualization on the process of goal achievement will be higher and you will achieve a goal sooner.

Early in the morning, right after you wake up, and late in the evening, right before you go to bed, are periods of time when visualization is most effective for activating the subconscious mind. Why? When you imagine your goal as achieved before going to sleep, you program your subconscious mind to think during the entire night about ideas that can help to achieve this goal. The subconscious mind works best during the night when the conscious mind is inactive, and if you visualize the goal before going to bed, you will come up with excellent ideas in the morning or later during the day. When you visualize a goal early in the morning you program your subconscious mind to think about ideas that can help to achieve your goal during the entire day. The earlier you first visualize a goal during the day for the first time, the sooner you activate your subconscious mind and the more ideas you will generate during the day that can be helpful to achieve a goal. Make it a habit to visualize goals after waking up and before going to bed because during these time frames activating the subconscious mind is especially powerful.

Visualize your goals frequently and clearly because this is what turns them into reality. Visualization is a magic wand that turns dreams into reality because it motivates actions, stimulates ideas and draws resources. When you work on the goal remember the visualization magic formula: clarity of visualization X frequency of visualization = achieved goal.

The secret to productive goal setting is in establishing clearly defined goals, writing them down and then focusing on them several times a day with words, pictures and emotions as if we've already achieved them. – Denis Waitley

Positive thinking

Law of attraction

Several years ago, I participated in an extreme driving course and one of the techniques I practiced was zigzag driving between obstacles. My instructor said: "Andrii, the car tends to drive towards the point you look at. Don't look at the next obstacle so you don't hit it. Look at the final destination you want to reach instead." The law of attraction says, "You get what you think about most of the time." This law has been used by successful people for thousands of years, it was described in numerous ancient manuscripts and because of its incredible power is often called the law of the universe.

Visualization is incredibly powerful because it instructs your subconscious about which resources to draw, which actions to take and which ideas to generate in order to bring more of what you think about to your life. Your brain will fulfill exactly what you tell it to do and every thought, whether positive or negative, will have an impact on your future. For example if you think, "I don't want to hit this obstacle in the road," you are likely to hit it; however, if you think, "I want to reach the destination safely," you will reach it safely because you draw what you think about. If you think "I have a big debt and it is terrible," you will draw even more financial problems to your life; however, if you think "I want to double my income this year," you will be likely to double it because you draw what you think about. If you think "I am afraid to fail during tomorrow's public presentation," you will be likely to fail; however, if you think "I will make a great presentation tomorrow," you will be likely to make a great presentation because you draw what you think about.

Successful people are extremely solution-oriented and think about how to achieve their dreams most of the time. Unsuccessful people on the contrary think about difficulties, worries and who to blame most of the time. Thoughts become reality, that's why it is important to visualize what you want to achieve rather than what you want to avoid. For example, imagine yourself being fit and healthy rather than worry about your extra weight. Take control of what you think about because your subconscious works as a thought amplifier and will ultimately turn into reality what you think about most of the time, whether it is something good or something bad.

Results you are experiencing in your life today are a reflection of thoughts you had yesterday. Change the balance between positive and negative thoughts in your head, and you will live the life of your dreams. How? Make a conscious decision to feed your brain with positive thoughts and to block negative thoughts.

Put your brain on a positive diet

Wear positive glasses

Imagine that you have won in a lottery and bought the car of your dreams. In the morning, you notice that somebody has scratched it in a parking lot. Although almost everything in your life is awesome, you might concentrate the majority of your time on a single bad thing – a scratch. When people have 99% good things and 1% bad things in their life they concentrate their attention on exactly 1% bad things. Because we get what we think about, these thoughts attract even more negative events in their lives and block everything that is good. The happiness and greatness of your future depends on your ability to concentrate your attention on the 99% good things in your life and to be happy about what you already have.

If you concentrate your attention on the 1% negative things in your life, you will draw negative events. If you think about and appreciate the 99% good things, you will draw positive events. You will get and achieve anything you want, once you learn to appreciate life. Be happy about everything you already have, about all the little things that surround you without any specific reason. "I am alive. And I am happy about it," "I have a computer and I am happy about it," "The sun is shining – awesome," "I will have lunch soon. Cool!" At first, you smile and think positively about the little good things that surround you deliberately and later this positive energy will draw everything you want. Successful people concentrate most of their time on what is good in their lives rather than what is bad in their lives.

Whether you expect bad things to happen in your life or good things to happen in your life, you will rarely be disappointed because we draw what we think about. Successful people always expect that something good will happen to them. Their attitude is: "The world is friendly to me. The world is full of resources and supports me on the way to my goals." Positive expectations of successful people according to the law of attraction draw necessary resources, ideas and events that help them to achieve their goals.

Focus your attention on things that are currently good in your life. Expect that great things will happen in your life in the future. Wearing positive glasses and being an optimist will significantly improve your positive and negative thoughts balance, which will draw happiness and success to your life. Behind your habit of seeing life through the positive lens lies success in all aspects of life: money, relationships, health and personal development.

Feed your brain with positive thoughts

Every thought, whether positive or negative, that comes to your mind will impact your life. Since we get what we think about most of the time, in order to change the ratio of positive to negative thoughts and draw success, deposit positive thoughts into your mind intentionally. Simply say to yourself regularly positive assertive statements about anything you want to be true and your performance and success will skyrocket.

For example, once you wake up you may think, "I will enjoy every minute of this day and it may be the best day of my life." During the day you can say to yourself, "I am drawing a huge amount of resources and ideas," "I am financially free and have as much money as I need," "I am a magnet for success and luck," "I am brimming with energy and am overflowing with joy," or "I possess the qualities needed to be extremely successful." Before going to bed you might say, "Creative energy surges through me and leads me to new and brilliant ideas," "I am happy about myself," and "Tomorrow I will have a very successful day."

Once you increase the number of positive thoughts that flow through your brain daily, you will draw ideas, resources and events that will help to make your dreams a reality. Once you increase the number of positive thoughts that flow through your brain daily, you will be energetic, cheerful and charismatic. Once you increase the number of positive thoughts that flow through your brain daily, you will become a happier person. As we draw what we think about most of the time, the nature of your dominant thoughts is a root cause of your success or failure. Being an optimist is lucrative because positive thinking brings much more success in life than negative thinking.

Glaring Sphere Technique

Glaring Sphere is an excellent technique that can amplify the power of positive thoughts and fill you with necessary energy for achievement of goals. Glaring Sphere is an excellent technique to do during "wasted time" such as taking a shower, waiting in line, jogging or walking to the parking lot. Glaring Sphere is one of the most powerful techniques in success psychology and I am sure it will bring you great results as it has brought to thousands of people worldwide

Tell yourself several positive statements that you want to be true. For example, "I attract money like a magnet," "I am incredibly successful," and "I am generating successful business ideas." Simultaneously imagine a little glaring sphere inside you that is full of qualities mentioned in the positive statements. In our example, the glaring sphere would be full of money magnetism, successfulness and creativity. In your mental picture, simultaneously increase the glare of the sphere and the concentration of qualities mentioned in the positive statements. Imagine how the sphere grows in size until it covers your entire body, then how it grows until it covers the entire room, then the entire city and finally the entire planet. After you clearly see a mental image of the glaring sphere full of qualities mentioned in the positive statements with a center inside you that covers the entire planet, the exercise is finished. Your subconscious clearly received your message and will do everything to draw what you want as much as possible to your life.

The Glaring Sphere technique allows you to at least mentally become a superman or a super woman and to gain qualities you need to achieve your dreams. And you know what the coolest part is? You can choose whatever qualities you want.

The following chain reaction occurs in our life: If you experience positive emotions today, they will create your tomorrow and tomorrow you will also experience positive emotions; if you experience positive emotions tomorrow, they will build your day after tomorrow and the day after tomorrow you will also experience positive emotions. Make yourself a rule to intentionally create positive emotions in your life by concentrating attention on positive things, expecting positive events to happen in the future and feeding your brain with positive thoughts. This habit will allow you to get into the flow of positive events and to make each subsequent day more joyful than the previous one.

Eliminate negative thoughts

Block negative thoughts

Your subconscious mind is programmed by your thoughts and is incredibly powerful in drawing what you think about most of the time to your life. However, with great power comes a great responsibility because the subconscious mind not only can bring good things to your life and make it happy, but also bring bad things to your life and make it miserable. Your brain will fulfill exactly what you tell it to do and every thought whether positive or negative will have an impact on your future.

For example, if you are trying to create a business and the following thoughts come to your mind, "I am not cut out for this," "I doubt it is possible," or "I am worth nothing," these negative thoughts will block your subconscious from generating ideas, will reduce your enthusiasm to take action, will prevent you from noticing valuable resources and at the first sign of difficulty you will throw a white flag and say to yourself: "You see, I was right when I said that I am not cut out for this, it's not possible and I am worth nothing." Every thought serves as a command for your subconscious to turn this thought into reality. If you think that you are poor, you are likely to become poorer, if you fear being fired you increase your chances of getting fired, if you doubt that you can achieve your goal, you become less likely to achieve it. Negative thoughts draw negative events and if they constitute the majority of thoughts in your head, they can literally make your life miserable. You might ask, "How can I protect myself from the negative thoughts then?"

Firstly, control thoughts that get into your head and once you notice that a particular thought is negative, for example, "I am poor," "I am unlucky," or "I don't have time," consciously block it. Tell yourself: "I won't let this thought poison my subconscious and make my life less awesome than it can be." Secondly, when you hear other people around you being pessimistic and discussing how something is bad or impossible, either avoid communicating with them or change the topic of the conversation. Negative thoughts that you hear from other people are toxic and dangerous poison because they can affect your own thoughts and results in life. Reduce the amount of negative thoughts that you hear from other people in private conversations, reduce the amount of negative thoughts that you hear from other people on TV, and reduce the amount of negative thoughts that you hear from other people on the internet.

Positive people have positive expectations in their lives and most of their days are successful. Negative people have negative expectations in their lives and most of their days are unsuccessful. By reducing the amount of negative thoughts that flow through your head, you can significantly improve your results in life. Enjoy your life today, only so you can make it even more awesome in the future.

React positively to both positive and negative events

Imagine that a colleague at work stole your wallet. After you had a conversation with your manager and the robber the wallet was returned. Despite a good end to the incident, you stay angry at the colleague for 2 more months and every negative thought that comes to your mind draws unpleasant events to your life. A bad event in your life isn't as dangerous as the flow of negative thoughts that it can activate in your head. It's the negative thoughts that make us unhappy and bring harm to ourselves, not the events.

The majority of people are used to reacting with positive thoughts to positive events and with negative thoughts to negative events. Once you develop a habit to react positively to both positive and negative events, you will get into the fast lane towards the life of your dreams because we draw what we think about most of the time. You might think, "How is it possible to react positively to negative events?"

Firstly, when people do bad things to you, always forgive them instantly and say to yourself, "I forgive this person and wish him or her well." Of course, you can take actions to prevent these people from doing bad things to you again or avoid communicating with them in the future, but you need to forgive them quickly to stop a flow of negative and destructive thoughts that may affect your future. When you forgive people it's not they who benefit, it's you who benefits.

Secondly, find something positive in every negative event and develop a mindset that everything that happens in your life can help you to fulfill your dreams in one way or another. For example: You failed in business – "That's OK, I learned a valuable lesson and will act better next time." You need to wait for 10 hours at the airport – "Excellent! I will have time to read an interesting book." Somebody swears at you – "I enjoy life, appreciate that most people around me don't swear and wish this person well."

Sure, unpleasant things that are out of your control occasionally happen, but there's one thing you always have control over – your reaction. If you think negatively about negative events you draw even more bad things to your life. Make a conscious decision to react positively to all negative events because of the following benefits: maintaining high self-confidence and motivation to take actions, programming your subconscious mind to think about solutions rather than problems and drawing good events. This decision can reduce the number of unpleasant experiences in your life to a minimum and make you incredibly successful in achievement of your goals.

Don't take opinions of other people to heart

When people hear about your goal and say, "It's impossible," "It's unrealistic," or "Here are ten reasons why it can't be achieved," thank them for their opinion, calculate the risks and never think about this feedback again. If you become really concerned about somebody saying "You can't," you will activate a flow of negative thoughts in your head which will block creativity, lower motivation, draw failures and eventually bury your dream. If having everyone believe in your idea was a requirement for success then nobody would ever be able to achieve anything. Even the most successful ideas in the world such as the telephone, radio and The Beatles band initially received negative feedback.

Associates of David Sarnoff replied to his request to invest in radio in 1921: "The wireless music box has no imaginable commercial value. Who would pay for a message sent to no one in particular?"

After the audition by The Beatles, the Decca Records executive gave his verdict to the band's manager: "Not to mince words, Mr. Epstein, but we don't like your boys' sound. Groups are out; four-piece groups with guitars particularly are finished."

Western Union officials who reviewed Alexander Graham Bell's offer to purchase his telephone patent wrote: "The Telephone purports to transmit the speaking voice over telegraph wires. We found that the voice is very weak and indistinct, and grows even weaker when long wires are used between the transmitter and receiver. Technically, we do not see that this device will ever be capable of sending recognizable speech over a distance of several miles. Messrs. Hubbard and Bell want to install one of their 'telephone devices' in every city. The idea is idiotic on the face of it. Furthermore, why would any person want to use this ungainly and impractical device when he can send a messenger to the telegraph office and have a clear written message sent to any large city in the United States?"

Negative opinions of people can't bury your dream, but your reaction to them can. Whenever you hear "You can't," thank the person for his or her opinion, calculate the risks and never think about it again because a flow of negative thoughts activated by your internal critic can be detrimental to your success.

Life is 10% what happens to you and 90% how you react to it. – Charles R. Swindoll

The Achievement Factory

You have to believe in yourself when no one else does. That's what makes you a winner. – Venus Williams, Olympic gold medalist and professional tennis champion

Strategy

A plan for achieving a goal

According to research by psychology professor Dr. Gail Matthews at Dominican University, people who just think about their goals achieve them with 43% probability. People who not only think about their goals but also write down their goals achieve them with 61% probability. But people who in addition to writing down goals, also create a plan with specific action items and regularly check progress, increase their chances for success to 76%. Of course these numbers may be different depending on circumstances and the nature of your goal, but one thing is certain: having a plan with clear action items is critical for making your dreams a reality.

If you develop a plan on how to achieve a goal, you create a map in your brain that shows the way towards the goal. With the map all actions you take will be aligned in the direction to the goal, and their individual positive effects will be combined. After you have clearly decided what goal you want to achieve and have written it down, develop an action plan.

Many years ago I asked a serial entrepreneur, multimillionaire and exceptional goal-achiever, "Jason, imagine that you want to launch a new business. How would you decide which actions to take first?" He replied, "Andrii, if I wake up in the morning and decide to become a chocolate producer, I break this complex task into several simpler ones: 'How can I produce tasty chocolates?' and 'How can I sell many chocolates?'

"Each of these problems I split into several even smaller problems. 'How can I produce tasty chocolates?' may be split into: 'How do I get a recipe for tasty chocolate?' and 'How do I outsource production of my chocolate?' The task, 'How can I sell many chocolates?' may be split into: 'How can I sell chocolates through supermarkets?' and 'How can I promote chocolates through media?'

"All tasks get split into smaller tasks until they get so small that by thinking about them, I can come to specific actions that need to be taken.

"I use this strategy every day for solving complex business tasks. Andrii, if you want to solve a complex problem, just build a pyramid from smaller problems and you will be able to solve tasks that seem unsolvable from the first glance."

To develop an action plan regularly ask yourself, "How can I achieve my goal?" or "What else can I do to make my dream a reality?" These questions will stimulate your subconscious mind to generate ideas of how to split achieving your big goal into sub goals and which particular action steps need to be taken to accomplish each of them. Write all ideas for action steps that you generate and consider valuable into the action plan. After you began a journey towards the goal, regularly update your plan taking into account new ideas you generate, obstacles you face and results you get because the best strategy is a flexible strategy.

For example, imagine that your goal is to be able to do 100 pull-ups at a time. You ask yourself, "How can I achieve my goal?" and get two ideas for the initial plan: "I need to install a bar at home" and "I need to find a training plan recommended by a person who can do more than 100 pull-ups." In 3 weeks, you increased the number of pull-ups that you can do but realized that you stopped making progress. You ask yourself, "What else can I do to make my dream a reality?" and update your plan with new ideas, "I need to switch the training plan to a more effective one" and "I need to also add pushups to my training that develop chest muscles necessary for pull-ups."

When, as a college student, I first went to the gym, I noticed guys who were carrying with them everywhere a paper with their workout plan. I thought, "Why do they bother writing this plan and don't just do random fitness exercises like me?" In a few months I realized that the guys with the best results in the gym were always these guys who carried a plan.

After you have clearly decided what you want and have written down your dream, create a plan with specific action items. Regularly measure your progress and based on the lessons you learn on the way to the goal and the results you achieve, update the plan. Developing a plan and regularly improving it is one of most important concepts that successful people use for achieving their goals.

Measure progress

In order to increase the effectiveness of the effort you make towards achieving a goal, measure progress regularly. There are two reasons why measuring progress is important.

The Achievement Factory

Firstly, progress is one of the best motivators in the world to take action, and the best way to recognize the progress towards the goal is to measure it. Imagine that you want to lose weight and begin weighing yourself every morning. When you stand on the scale and see the number that is lower than the one you saw yesterday, you experience a small success. When you experience success, dopamine, a happiness-inducing hormone, is released in the brain and as a result you feel joy. Guess what? You will do your best to eat less during the day and to exercise to experience joy from progress again. Regular progress measurement and intermediate celebrations will help you to not only achieve a goal but enjoy a process of achieving it.

Secondly, regular progress measurement week by week, day by day, or hour by hour will allow you to quickly identify where you are not progressing as you wanted. Successful people always know exactly where they are on the way to their goal and once they see that what they do hasn't been bringing them closer to the goal for a while, they quickly adjust their strategy.

To achieve a goal of any size you need to make measurable progress towards it every day. Measuring progress will allow you to stay motivated to take actions in the direction of the goal and know when you need to change a strategy if your progress stops or slows down. Decide whether to measure a progress by means of checklists, percentages, pounds, pages, dollars or any other means, and also which intermediate points you should go through on the way to the destination.

What's measured improves. — Peter F. Drucker

A perfect strategy is a flexible strategy

A famous French naturalist, Jean-Henri Fabre, conducted an interesting experiment with Pine Processionary caterpillars. He took several caterpillars and placed them in single file around the rim of a flowerpot. Each caterpillar's head touched the end of the caterpillar in front of it so that the procession formed a full circle. Fabre placed pine needles, which are the favorite food of the caterpillars of this type, in the middle of the circle formed by the procession. What makes a Processionary caterpillar special is the instinct to blindly follow the caterpillar in front of it. All caterpillars went in circles hour after hour, day after day, night after night thinking that the caterpillar in front of them was heading to the food. In 7 days, all the caterpillars died from hunger and exhaustion although food was just 6 inches away from them and the only thing they needed to do to get it was to change the direction of movement. The procession died simply because when the strategy of finding food didn't give results, the caterpillars didn't change it.

Millions of people who fail to achieve their goals follow the principle "It was always done here this way." Just like Processionary caterpillars, they do something actively every day, don't get results, but instead of changing their strategy continue doing what they were doing.

If you want to achieve your goal, the strategy you are using need not be clever or original but it should bring results. If you see that what you are doing isn't bringing results, simply change your approach. If that approach again doesn't produce results, keep changing it until what you do brings you closer to your goal.

Successful people know that the perfect strategy to achieve a goal is a flexible strategy that is constantly adjusted based on the results it brings. Do more of what works, do less of what doesn't and experiment to see if you can make your strategy even more effective. When you take actions in the direction of your desires, analyze your actions, improve your actions and change your actions, you will never stop making progress towards the life of your dreams.

For every failure, there's an alternative course of action. You just have to find it. When you come to a roadblock, take a detour. – Mary Kay Ash, founder of Mary Kay Cosmetics

When I was young I thought that people at the top really understood what the hell was happening … whether they were cardinals or bishops or generals or politicians or business leaders. They knew. Well, I'm up there, and now I know they don't know. – David Mahoney

One step closer to the goal

In 1977, at the age of only 18, Terry Fox was diagnosed with bone cancer and his right leg was amputated 6 inches above the knee. While staying at a hospital, Terry was so touched by the suffering of other patients (many of them young children) that he decided to run across Canada to raise money for cancer research. Within 143 days, Terry ran 3,339 miles across Canada with prosthesis at a rate of almost 26 miles per day. When asked how he managed to cover such an enormous distance, he said: "I just keep running to the next telephone pole."

The Achievement Factory

If you think about the amount of work that needs to be done to achieve a big goal, you may be scared even to begin. No matter how big your goal is, it is always achieved one step, one task and one measure at a time. If you always focus only on the next step that can get you closer to the goal, and make a little bit of progress every day, you will definitely achieve your dream. After you achieve it and look back on what you have accomplished, you will be amazed and proud of yourself.

Imagine that you are driving a car in a thick fog and can see only 10 yards in front of you. After you pass these 10 yards, you see the next 10 yards, and after you pass them yet another 10 yards. You don't see the entire way but by concentrating on the next 10 yards at each point in time, you will be able to cover any distance to your destination.

Often people have a dream but are afraid to start because they don't see the path completely and the outcome is uncertain. Achieving a big goal is often similar to driving in a thick fog because when you move towards your goal, you don't need to know the entire way but you just need to know how to take the next step. Once you have taken a step, you will see how to take a consequent step and if you keep moving you will eventually reach the destination.

No matter how huge your goal is and how unclear the path is that leads to it, you will always get from where you are to where you want to be if you focus on taking just one next step. Take this step, then a logical next step, and then yet another step and eventually you will realize that your dream becomes a reality. Ask yourself, "What can I do today to get at least one step closer to my dream?" and remember that an elephant is eaten one piece at a time.

The Achievement Factory

How to run an ultramarathon? Puff out your chest, put one foot in front of the other, and don't stop till you cross the finish line. – Dean Karnazes

A journey of a thousand leagues begins with a single step. – Lao Tzu

You don't try to build a wall. You don't set out to build a wall. You don't say, 'I'm going to build the biggest, baddest, greatest wall that's ever been built.' You don't start there. You say, 'I'm going to lay this brick as perfectly as a brick can be laid.' And then you do that every single day, and soon you have a wall. – Will Smith

Take massive action towards the goal

Law of inertia

During the winter when I was 12, I missed 2 weeks of ballroom dance classes due to illness. After I recovered and was supposed to go to the upcoming dance class, I realized that it was rather difficult to do. I thought, "I am a bit lazy today. I just don't feel like turning off the TV and going outside from the cozy apartment. I will miss just one more class." In a few days, just 15 minutes before I had to go to the dance school, I realized, "I am still lazy and don't want to go outside. If it requires so much effort to just leave the apartment today, how much effort it will require me to attend the dance school regularly?"

That day, I finally summoned up my willpower and forced myself to get out of the apartment. After the class I realized, "Wow! I enjoyed all 1.5 hours of the class. I learned 3 new movements and I feel very energetic. How awesome it is that I finally went to the class. I love dancing!" After that day I attended the dance school regularly again, it didn't take me any effort or willpower to get out of the apartment and I never missed a class before the summer break. After the summer break in September, just before going to the first dance class of the school year, I realized that it was rather difficult to do. I thought, "I am a bit lazy today. If I miss just one class it probably won't be a big deal." I learned that if I attend dance classes regularly it's easy and enjoyable to continue attending them, but if I miss several classes in a row it requires a huge effort to begin attending them again.

Newton's Law of Motion or Law of Inertia says, "An object at rest stays at rest and an object in motion stays in motion with the same speed and in the same direction <u>unless acted upon by an unbalanced force.</u>" What this law essentially says is that it takes much less effort to maintain motion than to begin motion from a state of rest.

For example, a car consumes much more fuel to begin movement than to maintain movement, that's why fuel consumption in a traffic jam is higher than on a highway. Although Newton originally stated his law for physical movement, it also very well applies to movement towards our goals. Just like a car, you spend much more energy to take a first step towards your goal than to keep moving towards the goal.

"Many people think, if I feel so lazy to even begin taking action, how miserable it will be to go through the entire way to the goal?" Actually, on the way to the goal over 50% of effort is spent to just take a first step in its direction. Once you take the first step no matter how small and build a momentum, it will be easy for you to maintain movement towards the goal.

If you want to learn how to dance, go to the dance school and attend the first class. If you want to start a business, generate 100 business ideas during the brainstorming session. If you want to travel around the world, choose an exact route and estimate the cost. One of the most important things in achieving any goal is just to begin.

In numerous studies, psychologists have observed that people have a tendency to feel discomfort if they have started the task, but not finished it, the so-called Zeigarnik effect. In one research study, participants were given "brain buster" tasks and were interrupted before they could complete them. Although the participants were told to stop, nearly 90% of them finished the task anyway. Due to the Law of Inertia, people tend to procrastinate to take the first step towards their goals, but once it's taken they tend to finish what they have started because if they don't, due to the Zeigarnik effect they will experience discomfort.

Remember that if you want to achieve a goal, your main task is to simply take a first step. One step, no matter how small, may be enough to keep you moving towards the goal and make sure you don't stop until you achieve it.

You don't have to be great to get started, but you have to get started to be great. – Les Brown

Take massive directed action now

A few years ago, I met a highly successful entrepreneur and millionaire named John. John shared with me the following story: "When I was a student, I wanted very much to become a sales associate to earn my first paycheck. I went into the shopping mall, walked along the line of the apparel boutiques, entered each of them and asked, 'Who can I talk to about a job as a sales associate? Do you need a sales associate?' At the third boutique that I entered, a manager asked, 'Where did you see our job advertisement?' I smiled and said, 'I was just walking along the line of apparel boutiques, and decided to ask if you have an opening.' Although my approach surprised the manager, he interviewed me immediately. In half an hour I had a second interview with a senior manager and eventually received a job offer. Between the time I entered the shopping mall and the time I got a job, three hours elapsed. Had I known that I should write a résumé, prepare for the interview and have previous sales experience, my job search would have probably taken much, much longer."

Successful people know that the only thing you have control over is your own actions and to achieve a goal you need to take massive action. The more actions you take and the more seeds you plant, the bigger crop of results you will eventually gather and the sooner you will achieve your goal. Successful people are extremely action-oriented. Rather than spending excessive time on developing a plan and talking, they take a plunge, take massive action and correct their strategy along the way.

People often say, "I haven't taken a first step towards my goal because I am waiting for more favorable circumstances" or "I am waiting until I have more money" or "I am waiting until I get a better education." Remember that the perfect time to achieve your biggest goal is right now. The perfect resources to achieve the goal are those you have today. Instead of planning too long, thinking too long or waiting for the most favorable circumstances, take the first step towards the goal right now. You will realize that new opportunities, ideas and resources come to you not while you are waiting for them, but while you are taking actions towards the goal.

Be truthful to yourself: nothing will happen on its own, nobody will pull you anywhere, and complaints never help. If you want to get warmth from the oven you need to constantly feed it with firewood. Life works exactly like an oven, you first need to take action before you can see the results and experience joy, and to see a lot of results and experience a lot of joy regularly you need to take massive action daily. The amount of action you take is correlated with the progress you make, the amount of goals you achieve and the joy you experience.

The only thing that can make your life better is your own actions. The sooner you take a first step and the more actions you take regularly, the faster you will drive on the highway towards the life of your dreams.

Too many people spend too much time trying to perfect something before they actually do it. Instead of waiting for perfection, run with what you got, and fix it along the way. – Paul Arden

The one requirement for success in our business lives is effort. Either you make the commitment to get results or you don't. – Mark Cuban

Talent is cheaper than table salt. What separates the talented individual from the successful one is a lot of hard work. – Stephen King

Focus attention

What you focus your attention on is where your energy flows and what eventually gets done. Once you focus your attention on the goal, your mind generates ideas relevant to this goal and you take actions relevant to this goal. If you focus your attention on something else, you think about something else and take actions relevant to something else.

We always make choices of where to focus our attention and if you think about the past, you will notice that the most successful areas of your life are those where you have focused your attention the most. What gets your attention is eventually done. If you focus your attention on jogging, you jog. If you focus your attention on a phone conversation, you talk. If you focus your attention on your business, you generate business ideas or take actions that will develop it.

If you are not moving closer to your goal or your progress is slow, it simply means that you have decided to focus your attention elsewhere. In order to live the life of your dreams and fulfill your desires, you need to take necessary actions, and in order to take them you first need to focus your attention on your desires and the longer the better. If you make a conscious decision to focus attention as much as possible on the goal, you will take more necessary actions, generate more necessary ideas and achieve it sooner.

The American Journal of Experimental Psychology reported a study in which students spent approximately 40% longer on solving difficult math problems if they had to occasionally switch to other tasks. Another study done by Gloria Mark, an "interruption scientist" at the University of California, revealed that people who often switch between tasks work faster, but less productively. Both these studies showed that people who multitask not only are less productive than those who work on a single task at a time, but also experience a significantly higher level of stress, frustration and workload.

Very often if you recall how your day was spent, you might say, "I drank coffee, talked to a colleague, watched videos on the Internet, checked emails, read the news, talked on the phone and worked in between." All these distracters not only reduce the time you work during the day, but also make you much less productive during the time you actually work because as studies show, work with interruptions is less productive than work without interruptions.

How can you increase productivity and reduce the amount of stress while you take actions necessary to achieve your goal? Cut out all distracters such as social networks, phone calls or instant messaging and focus your attention completely on a single task for 30, 45 or 60 minutes without interruption, so that your entire energy is directed at it. When you dive into the task, forget about what happens around you and about all other activities, you will be much more productive. This state of focus, involvement and concentration gives hyper results. If you stop multitasking and practice single tasking, you will not only become significantly more productive but will also have much less stress in your life.

In order to achieve a goal you need to take actions. If you consciously decide to focus your attention on your goal as much as possible, it will guarantee that you take enough actions and will eventually achieve the goal. To make the time that you spend working towards the goal most productive and enjoyable, concentrate on a single task for 30, 45 or 60 minutes with minimum amount of interruptions.

My success is due more to my ability to work continuously on one thing without stopping than to any other single quality. – Thomas Edison

I've learned that only through focus can you do world-class things, no matter how capable you are. – Bill Gates

Concentrate all your thoughts upon the work at hand. The sun's rays do not burn until brought to a focus. – Alexander Graham Bell

Set a deadline

Two days before an exam, college students are perhaps the most productive people in the world. They cut out all entertainment, phone calls, social networks and focus entirely on exam preparation. Before the exam, they often study more than 16 hours per day with extremely high productivity. Why does this happen? They think, "I have a very strict deadline that is very close. I really want to pass the exam and I have no other options than to prepare within just two days." The reason for students' super-productivity is the deadlines.

Deadlines develop a sense of urgency and make your internal voice periodically say, "The deadline you have to meet is close. Focus your attention and energy entirely on the goal. Take action without procrastination." Deadlines force your subconscious mind to generate ideas more effectively. Deadlines are the tool that allows you to increase attention, focus on the task you want to accomplish and achieve more goals in less time.

For each goal you want to achieve, even if you don't know exactly how you will achieve it, set a firm deadline. For example, "I will be able to do 25 pull-ups by October 21" or "I will create a website for my company within 2 months." Once you begin moving in the direction of the goal and learn new information, you may adjust the deadline if necessary.

In order for the deadline to help you to increase productivity, make sure that it is realistic in your mind however with a stretch. For example, if you decide to lose 20 pounds in 2 days, you won't believe that you can do that and won't take any action at all to achieve this goal. If you decide to lose 20 pounds in 10 years, you will procrastinate taking any actions because the deadline is very far away. However, if you decide to lose 20 pounds in 3 months, you will believe that it is possible and also have a sense of urgency to take action right now in order to meet the deadline.

You might reasonably ask, "What should I do if I don't meet the deadline?" Of course if you miss the deadline, you shouldn't stop pursuing your goal, but just set a new deadline and continue working on the goal until you achieve it. Make sure that for each goal and sub goal you set a realistic deadline, however with a stretch that will create an internal pressure to take massive action without procrastination and to do your best to achieve a goal as quickly as possible. This technique gives hyper results in little time.

Failures and persistence

Failures are your friends

In order to become a great dancer you first need to do a movement incorrectly, then correct yourself and improve your movement. In order to become a great violin player you first need to play a composition incorrectly, then correct yourself and play it better the next time. In order to become a successful entrepreneur you first need to fail, learn why what you did didn't work out and then change your approach. High achievers know that in order to achieve a goal, you need to make good decisions. Good decisions come from experience and experience comes from failures. When you fail, you learn what doesn't work and why. This experience is the reason why you eventually succeed.

Professor Dean Keith decided to explore the relationship between the quantity and quality of ideas. He studied the work of hundreds of the most creative scientists and made a very interesting discovery. The best scientists created more successful ideas than the mediocre ones. However, the best scientists also created many more bad ideas than the mediocre scientists.

The vast majority of papers written by the world's most famous scientists were never cited. A small percentage of them received a little over 100 citations and only several papers had an incredible impact on the world. Professor Keith has done the same study with composers and other fine artists and found that the more bad ideas a composer, a scientist or an artist generated, the more successful ideas he or she had.

Thomas Edison filed over 2,000 patents, but the majority of them didn't make him a cent. Albert Einstein published over 300 scientific papers, but the majority of them are not cited by other scientists. Pablo Picasso created more than 20,000 pieces of art, but most of them are not presented at the best art exhibitions. There is a direct correlation between quantity and quality of ideas. The majority of ideas that the best idea creators generate are bad, some of them are average and very few are genius. These few genius ideas make the best creators enormously successful.

When Walt Disney was seeking funding for Disneyland in Anaheim, California, he was rejected by 302 bankers before he received the necessary funding. James Dyson created 5,126 failed prototypes before creating a working version of a dual-cyclone bagless vacuum cleaner. R.H. Macy started seven failed businesses before finally creating Macy's department store in New York City and making billions of dollars.

Successful people fail far more often than other people and the size of their success is proportional to the number of failures they make. Successful people are hungry for failures because they know that the more they fail, the more they learn, the more they learn, the better they act, and the better they act, the sooner they succeed. Perceive failures as an essential component of success and instead of being scared of failures, double your failure rate because a life without failures is a life without achievement and a life without achievement is a life without happiness.

It doesn't matter how many times you fail. It doesn't matter how many times you almost get it right. No one is going to know or care about your failures, and neither should you. All you have to do is learn from them and those around you because... All that matters in business is that you get it right once. Then everyone can tell you how lucky you are. – Mark Cuban

Unless you're not pushing yourself, you're not living to the fullest. You can't be afraid to fail, but unless you fail, you haven't pushed hard enough. – Dean Karnazes

The person interested in success has to learn to view failure as a healthy, inevitable part of the process getting to the top. – Dr. Joyce Brothers

Life's persistence test

In 1867 one of the best engineers of his time, John Roebling, decided to build a spectacular suspension bridge that would connect Brooklyn with Manhattan in New York. As there was no bridge of such magnitude ever built before, engineers around the world said, "Building a bridge of this type is impossible. Forget this idea." Despite the opinions of colleagues, John Roebling wholeheartedly believed that he could build the bridge of his dreams. The only person who shared John's vision was his son Washington, who at that time was an upcoming engineer. Together they created a detailed plan, hired a crew and started working on the bridge with a lot of enthusiasm.

A few months after a tragic accident at the site in 1869, John died and Washington took charge of the entire project. Fate was so cruel that shortly after Washington took charge of the bridge, as a result of construction-related decompression sickness, his body was completely paralyzed. He wasn't able to walk or talk and the only body part that he could move was one finger. The experts who said before the project started that building a bridge of this type was impossible now said, "Remember how we said that starting this project was totally unreasonable? John and Washington Roebling are crazy fools!"

Most people would certainly give up at this point but Washington, although handicapped, was determined to accomplish building the bridge, even though he didn't know how yet. One day an idea came to Washington while he was lying on his hospital bed: "Hey, the only thing I can do is move one finger. I will develop a code to communicate with my wife by moving a single finger!"

Thus Washington developed a code that allowed him to communicate with his wife, Emily, by tapping with his finger on her arm. For 13 years, Emily interpreted Washington's instructions for engineers and helped to supervise the construction until the bridge was finally completed in 1883. Whenever you are pursuing your dream and a thought of "Should I give up or should I persist?" comes to your mind, remember the story of the Brooklyn Bridge, the bridge that was built by one finger.

People often blame external circumstances and obstacles for their inactivity. The Brooklyn Bridge story demonstrates that no matter what the circumstances are, if you persist you will always achieve your goal. The external circumstances can't stop you, the only thing that can stop you is the limitations you create in your head, yourself. Obstacles are as essential a part of the process of fulfilling dreams as rain is an essential part of the weather. When rain starts you don't blame the rain, but simply pull out an umbrella; when you face an obstacle don't blame the obstacle but just constructively look for a way to overcome it.

Successful people fall down, pick themselves up and try again, over and over again before they pass life's "persistence test" and achieve what they want. Thomas Edison once said: "When I have fully decided that a result is worth getting, I go ahead of it and make trial after trial until it comes. Nearly every man, who develops an idea, works it up to the point where it looks impossible, and then gets discouraged. That's not the place to become discouraged." Remember that success is a game of character and defeat is not possible as long as you don't stop trying to achieve a goal and continue to move forward.

History has demonstrated that the most notable winners usually encountered heartbreaking obstacles before they triumphed. They won because they refused to become discouraged by their defeats. – B.C. Forbes, founder of Forbes magazine

I can summarize the lessons of my life in seven words – never give in; never, never give in. – Winston Churchill

I do not think there is any other quality so essential to success of any kind, as the quality of perseverance. It overcomes almost everything, even nature. – John D. Rockefeller, at one time the richest self-made man in the world

The difference in winning and losing is most often, not quitting. – Walt Disney

Fuel for achieving goals

Burning desire to achieve a goal

In 1979 James Dyson bought one of the most advanced vacuum cleaners on the market, and after using it got frustrated with how quickly it clogged and began losing suction. James got excited about this problem and decided, "I will design a vacuum cleaner that will clean the house more effectively."

Partly supported by the salary of his wife, who worked as an art teacher, and partly by bank loans, James spent almost 5 years working on his vacuum cleaner design and after 5,126 failed prototypes eventually created a working version of a dual-cyclone bagless vacuum cleaner. In a few years, the Dyson vacuum cleaner became one of the most desirable household appliances worldwide and James Dyson became a billionaire.

People often wonder about persistence of successful people and their ability to overcome obstacles. When you want to drive from point A to point B you need enough fuel in the tank. No matter how powerful your car is, without enough fuel you will never reach your destination. The same is true with goal setting. If you want to fulfill your desire, you need to have enough motivation inside, or you will never reach it.

What motivated James Dyson to continue working on the bagless vacuum cleaner after 5,000 failed prototypes? What motivated Walt Disney to pursue his dream after 300 banks refused to give him a loan for building Disneyland? What motivated Agatha Christie to continue writing after 5 years of rejections from publishing houses?

At an early age, children are taught to use PUSH motivation to achieve goals. PUSH motivation is when you take action because of your discipline, willpower or fear of punishment. In childhood, we get most of our goals from adults. A teacher says, "Do your homework," parents say, "Clean your room," a trainer says, "Do 10 pull-ups." You think, "I don't want to do my homework (or clean my room or do 10 pull-ups) but I will PUSH myself and do it." PUSH motivation works well for small short-term goals that are set in front of you by somebody else. However, PUSH motivation doesn't last long and doesn't bring big results. When people grow up and set their own goals they, out of habit, often continue to use PUSH motivation. The use of PUSH motivation is the biggest reason why people fail to achieve goals and to live the lives of their dreams.

The reason why James Dyson, Walt Disney, Agatha Christie and millions of other people achieved their goals is that they used the motivation of DESIRE. Motivation of DESIRE is when you take actions not because of fear, not because you have a strong willpower or discipline but because you have a burning desire to achieve a goal and this motivation is thousands times more powerful than PUSH motivation.

In order to achieve amazing goals, you need a lot of energy and your burning desire is the source of this energy. The amount of this energy is proportional to the intensity of desire. The bigger the goal you want to achieve, the more intense your desire should be to get from where you are to where you want to be. Burning desire is the huge power that will give you energy to complete the necessary work, overcome obstacles and endure failures on the way to the goal.

When you have a burning desire to achieve a goal, you feel goose bumps even by thinking about your future. When you have a burning desire to achieve a goal, you feel as if a part of you is dying if you are not pursuing it. When you have a burning desire, you wake up in the morning excited to take a couple of more steps in the direction of the goal.

People who don't have enough motivation are likely to give up once they face the first difficulties on the way to the goal. But when you want something very, very, very much, the conversation that happens in your head usually sounds like, "Hey, I feel miserable after failure. Maybe quitting is a good option? But I very much want to create this vacuum cleaner." "Maybe, let's do something less stressful, this goal is not for you? But I want to create this vacuum cleaner very much, and won't feel OK unless I achieve it. Maybe postpone it for better times? But I want it very much."

I noticed that if I wanted something really badly I always got it. There was not a single situation in my life, my wife's life, my students' lives and the lives of people I ever had a conversation with when we wanted something really badly and didn't get it. Do you know why this happens? It happens because the power of motivation of DESIRE is so huge, that no matter how unachievable the goal seems, it will get you to your destination guaranteed.

When you want something but still don't have it then you either don't really want it, or don't want it badly enough.

Why? Because if you wanted it badly enough you would either already have achieved your goal, or be busy working on the way to achieving it. After researching thousands of people and their lives, I realized that if you have a burning desire to achieve a goal you will always achieve it, and figuring out how to do so isn't difficult. What is truly difficult for most people is to set goals that they would have a burning desire to achieve.

Desire is such a powerful engine that it will always get you from where you are to where you want to be. If you want your goal to be achieved, your desire to achieve it should be intense. And for the desire to be intense, your goal should include a big "What," big "Why" and big "Want."

Nothing great was ever achieved without enthusiasm. – Ralph Waldo Emerson

The starting point of all achievement is DESIRE. Keep this constantly in mind. Weak desire brings weak results, just as a small fire makes a small amount of heat. – Napoleon Hill

The only way to do great work is to love what you do. – Steve Jobs

Big What

As I am writing these words, in front of me is a book by Donald Trump with the title *Think Big and Kick Ass*. I like this title very much because it succinctly summarizes the secret of successful people, "Dream big and do the necessary work to achieve your goal." Successful people set big goals, not because they are so self-confident, not because they are greedy or insane, but because they know that big goals have much more energy behind them than small goals. If the goal is big for you, your desire to achieve it will also be big and as a result you will be much more likely to do the necessary work to achieve it.

At the age of 22, I set a goal to receive a Master of Business Administration degree. I realized, "The average candidate is 28 years old and has at least 5 years of experience in finance, supply chain management, marketing or strategy which I don't." In order to increase my chances, I decided to apply to 4 top 10 MBA programs in the U.S. where I had a burning desire to study, 2 second-tier schools in the U.S. and 1 school in the Ukraine. I thought, "Even if I fail to get accepted to a top MBA program I will definitely get accepted to one of the backup options."

In the winter, there was an event in Kyiv called "World MBA Tour" to which came admission officers and graduates from business schools from all over the world including top 10 MBA programs in the U.S. When I talked to representatives of these schools I felt goose bumps, I felt joy, and I felt excitement. On the way home it hit me, "Even a thought about one of the top 10 MBA programs in the U.S. makes me happy, even a thought about studying there gives me a huge amount of energy to do any work and overcome any obstacles. However, when I imagine myself studying at one of my backup options I feel no inspiration, no desire to do any work, no satisfaction. I realized that just getting an MBA degree wasn't a big enough goal for me to have a burning desire to achieve it, so I changed the goal slightly to "I want to receive a Master of Business Administration degree from one of the top 10 MBA programs in the U.S." Although this goal seemed impossible for me at the beginning, eventually I became the youngest person in the MBA program at the University of Michigan Ross School of Business.

Big dreams have big energy behind them. Big dreams motivate us to do things that we will never do for small dreams. Big dreams make our lives happier. When the goal isn't big enough, the desire to achieve it is low. When the goal isn't big enough, it's very easy to give up at the first sign of difficulties. When the goal isn't big enough, it's very difficult to persist no matter what.

Don't compromise your dreams, and settle for backup options, because in order to wake up every morning inspired, in order to have motivation to do necessary work and to overcome obstacles on the way to the goal, your goal needs to be BIG. Not BIG for your relatives, not BIG for your colleagues, not BIG for society but BIG for you. The goal should be big enough to stretch you, but not too huge to make it impossible to achieve.

My interest in life comes from setting myself huge, apparently unachievable challenges and trying to rise above them. – Sir Richard Branson

People are not lazy, they simply have impotent goals…that is…goals that do not inspire them. – Anthony Robbins

Dream big dreams; only big dreams have the power to move men's souls. – Marcus Aurelius, Roman emperor

Big Want

In our life we pursue many goals that other people say we should achieve. A manager says, "You should finish this report." Parents say, "You should clean your room," a teacher says, "You should do your homework," an advertisement says, "You should own an expensive car," society says, "You should have a secure job," and your friends say, "You should have your own house."

One of the biggest reasons people don't live the lives of their dreams is because they forget that the most important goals come not from external sources but from within. There is very little energy behind goals that other people set in front of us. When you work towards them, you experience laziness, you feel unmotivated, you don't persist and even once you achieve them it doesn't bring you satisfaction.

It's very easy to determine if the goal is your own by the words that you are using. If you say "I SHOULD have a nice car" then, most probably, you received this goal from external sources such as an advertisement, your friends or your spouse. If you say, "I WANT to have a nice car" then it's your own goal. Even though we don't notice it, when we refer to the goal that we truly want to achieve we use the word "Want" rather than "Should." If the goal is your OWN, then you will wake up excited to take necessary actions to achieve it but if the goal is not yours, you will be lazy. You can't get to the life of your dreams by achieving "Should" goals, but you can by achieving "Want" goals.

One of the secrets to happiness is to make sure that the majority of goals that you work towards are your OWN "I want" goals that are meaningful for you. Set goals that you want yourself, not the ones you pursue to please someone else or that others consider meaningful. The only way to get enough energy to do the necessary work, overcome obstacles and endure failures on the way to the goal is to have a burning desire to achieve it, and it's possible to have a burning desire to achieve a goal only if it's your OWN goal.

For example, when I decided to get an MBA degree at one of the top 10 universities in the U.S. it was my own goal. My mother thought that it was a bad idea, my friends said that taking a huge loan for education was insane, and none of my colleagues at work had an MBA degree from one of the top 10 schools in the U.S. or wanted one. This goal was my OWN goal and this is one of the main reasons why I managed to achieve it. If the goal matters deeply to you, there is no obstacle that could stop you on the way to achieving it. If the goal is your OWN, you will protect it, you will fight for it, you will battle for it, you will stand up for it and you will respect it.

Big Why

To make yourself truly desire to achieve a goal, you need to have a clear answer to the question, "Why is this goal important to me?" One of the biggest reasons why people don't achieve their goals is that their "Why" isn't big enough. A compelling reason why is what provides motivation to take actions towards what you want, to overcome obstacles and endure failures. Your "Why" should consist of the two biggest motivators of human beings: a pleasurable reward for

The Achievement Factory

achieving the goal and a painful consequence for not achieving it.

Firstly, imagine how your life will look like after you achieve your goal. List all the potential great things that you will experience once your desire is fulfilled. The more reasons you have and the more compelling they are, the bigger your desire will be to achieve a goal. The more desire you have, the more likely you are to get off the couch, do the necessary work and eventually achieve a goal. For example, if my goal is "I want to be able to do 50 pull-ups in 60 days," the potential benefits may be:

- I will look extremely fit and will be proud of my body.
- I will be able to record a video of myself doing 50 pull-ups and receive compliments from my friends.
- I will lose weight on the way to achieving my goal.
- In my childhood, I was never able to do more than 10 pull-ups on the bar, but always envied guys who could do tricks on the bar. Once I can do 50 pull-ups, I will be strong enough to learn tricks on the bar and fulfill my childhood dream.

Secondly, think about how your life will look like if your goal isn't achieved. List all the negative consequences if you don't fulfill your desire. Then amplify these negative consequences in your imagination, increase the feeling of pain and hate your future life without a fulfilled goal. For example, if your goal is "I want to lose 20 pounds by jogging on a treadmill and eliminating sweets from my diet within 3 months," a list of negative consequences of not reaching the goal may look like this:

- If I don't lose weight now, I might gain 30 more pounds within the next 3 years. I will look so ugly that my wife or husband will be ashamed to walk next to me.
- People with extra weight are more likely to get sick. I will suffer more diseases and will eventually die young.
- I won't have enough energy to do a great job in my business or in the company I work for. Eventually I won't self-realize or bring any value to the world and will be a failure.
- I will feel depressed and no amount of sweets will be able to make me any happier.

You can also make a consequence of not achieving a goal even more painful intentionally to increase your internal motivation to achieve it. For example, if your goal is to lose weight – wear clothes every day that you wore when you were much thinner. The discomfort from wearing clothes that are small will motivate you to lose weight quicker. Or make a commitment to people you respect that you will lose 20 pounds within 3 months. The pain from breaking your word and listening to their comments if you don't achieve a goal may motivate you even further.

Finally, make sure that both rewards and negative consequences are important and meaningful for you. The only goal of these pleasurable rewards and painful consequences is to evoke emotions in you, increase your desire to achieve a goal and motivate you to take action. Entice yourself with pleasurable rewards and scare yourself with negative consequences. If your "Why" is big enough for you, you will have such a burning desire to achieve a goal that you will do whatever it takes and no matter which obstacles you face on the way, you will achieve it sooner or later.

Emotional visualization test

A great way to check if you desire to achieve a particular goal badly enough is by using the emotional visualization test. Imagine as clearly as possible the moment when you have already achieved your goal. Clearly imagine what you see, hear and smell. Pay attention to how your body reacts. Do you feel happier? Do you feel excitement? Do you feel an internal smile? If yes, then you truly have a burning desire to achieve this goal and there are no walls that could stop you.

If you want to achieve a goal only in your head, chances are you don't have a burning desire to achieve it. You can deceive your head, but you can't deceive your body. If you don't have a burning desire to achieve a goal, your body will resist and scream, "Stop, this goal isn't yours. Don't take any actions to achieve it as you will waste time and effort but achievement of the goal won't bring you any joy."

This emotional test is a simple and effective way to test how important the goal is for you. In order to achieve a goal, you need to do a certain amount of work. And you will be motivated to do this work if your desire to achieve a goal is strong enough. Strong desire to achieve a goal evokes positive emotions even when you visualize a moment when it is achieved. A burning desire to achieve a goal will evoke emotions in you and these emotions are the fuel for your internal engine and drive your actions. If the goal evokes positive emotions, you will wake up excited. If the goal evokes positive emotions, you will feel goose bumps even by thinking about it. If the goal evokes positive emotions, you will feel an internal urge to take massive action to make your dream a reality.

In order for you to have a burning desire to achieve a goal, this goal should influence your emotions, as emotions are our main motivator. The goal that has a big What, a big Want and a big Why has a much bigger influence on emotions than a goal that doesn't and hence, has a much higher chance of being achieved. Listen to the voice of your body and test all your goals by the emotional visualization test. If a goal passes this test and you have strong enough desire to achieve it, you will not only definitely achieve the goal, but also the achievement of this goal will bring joy and happiness to your life.

When you are driving a car and want to get from one place to another, the two main things you need are clarity of what the destination is and enough fuel in the tank. If you want to achieve a goal, you also need to know exactly what it is and to have enough motivation inside. If you don't have enough desire to achieve a goal at the beginning of your trip, you will not only be unlikely to reach it but also will have no joy from reaching it.

You must have an intense, burning desire to achieve a goal in order to have enough internal fuel for the "vehicle" that will get you from where you are to where you want to be and you will have it if your goal has a big "What," a big "Why" and a big "Want."

Enjoy what you do as an exciting game

In the 1960s, Srully Blotnick, a PhD and psychologist, conducted a study of 1,500 people who wanted to become wealthy. He split them into two categories. Category A consisted of 1,245 people who said: "I am going to pursue money first and follow my passion later." Category B consisted of 255 people who said: "I am going to do what I am passionate about and trust that the money will follow later."

In 20 years, 101 people from the entire group became millionaires. What's interesting is that 100 millionaires were from Group B, where people specified following their passion as a first priority rather than money, and only 1 millionaire was from Group A. The group that consisted of only 17% studied accounted for 99% of the millionaires. Why is doing what you enjoy that important for achieving goals?

Everyone has the inner guidance system that tells you if you are working towards the right goal by the amount of joy you are experiencing in the process. Successful people always do what they love, because doing what you love is much more powerful fuel on the way to the goal than willpower. Work takes a significant amount of time in your life and if you enjoy what you do every day, you will not only achieve extraordinary results, but will also live a happy life.

If you enjoy what you do, you are much more likely to accomplish the amount of work necessary to achieve a goal, you wake up with anticipation to make progress and are very productive during the day, and you have a burning desire to act and perceive what you do as an exciting game, rather than a painful duty.

Make achieving goals a game

Psychologists have discovered that we are most productive when we are simultaneously relaxed, excited, open, confident, lively and playful. This state is called a high-performance state. What's interesting is that every time we are playing a game we are in a high-performance state. Hence, if you perceive the work you do as a game, you will do it with the highest performance.

Our attention is drawn to what is exciting and if you are doing a boring activity, you will be constantly distracted by things that are more interesting such as social media, computer games or chatting with friends. Find ways to make every task an entertaining game and you will not only enjoy your work more but also your productivity will grow significantly. For example, "I am checking how quickly I can finish these reports," "While running, I am listening to an interesting training on my Mp3 player" and "Let's see if I can accomplish more during the next hour than during the previous one."

Just like a car needs fuel to get from Point A to Point B, we need motivation to get from where we are to the desired goal. Enjoying what you do is one of the most powerful motivators in the world and can get you much further than willpower.

It is very hard to succeed in something unless you take the first step – which is to become very interested in it. – Warren Buffett

Success breeds success

Several years ago, while attending a conference in Las Vegas, I decided to have lunch in a cafeteria near a casino. At the door a lady asked, "Do you want to receive a 10% lunch discount? You can fill out this form to receive a free casino gambler's card that will allow you to both play at the casino and to receive a cafeteria discount." I said, "Sure, why not?" After I filled out the form, a casino representative took me to the 25¢ gambling machine and said, "Here is your card that is already preloaded with $3. After you play 12 times and use this $3 entirely, the card will be activated for use in the casino and cafeteria." I played 12 times, won $80 and the representative handed me the win in cash right away. I thought, "I went to the cafeteria to spend $15 on lunch but received not only a discount but also $80 in cash. What's the catch?"

During the conference I met David, who worked at a casino in the past, and he explained, "Andrii, the casino lets you win at the beginning to make you play longer and spend more money. Imagine that you came to the casino for the first time. You make a bet and lose. You make a second bet and lose. After you make a third bet and lose you say, 'Hey, it's impossible to win. It doesn't make sense to continue playing.' But what if you come to the casino for the first time and win several times in a row? Firstly, winning is pleasurable and you are motivated to experience this feeling again and again. Secondly, this success builds up your confidence that winning is possible. This self-confidence and motivation will allow you to persist in playing even after a long sequence of losses. You will think, 'Hey, I won in the past and it was pleasurable.

I can and I want to win again. The past losses are only temporary.'"

Achieving goals is similar to gambling and the more you succeed, the more you are motivated to succeed again and the more confident you are that succeeding is possible. After you achieve even a small goal, this small success will bring you to bigger success and bigger success will lead to a huge success and success grows like a snowball.

Every time you successfully reach a goal no matter how small, you make a contribution to your self-confidence and motivation piggy bank and tell yourself, "You see, I can succeed." The more success you experienced in the past, the higher is your confidence that you can overcome obstacles and sustain a long row of failures on the way to success. The more success you experienced in the past, the more pleasurable emotions you have experienced and the more motivation you have to experience even bigger success in the future because pleasurable emotions are addictive.

Just like in a casino, in order to do the necessary work to achieve a goal and win, you need to first experience small success in order to fill your self-confidence and motivation piggy bank and have a conviction: "I have succeeded in the past and also want and can succeed this time." Do you know why the probability of millionaires who went bankrupt to become millionaires again is many times higher than that of the average person? Because millionaires remember their past success, they have high confidence that becoming a millionaire is possible, and this confidence allows them to persist longer than a person who has never succeeded financially. Because millionaires remember their past success, unlike the average person they know that experiencing success is very pleasurable and the goal achievement is worth the effort. High achievers have bigger muscles for achieving goals than the majority of other people, because they train them by achieving goals of different sizes regularly.

Pursuing a big goal might be difficult at the beginning, but after you achieve a few initial successes, the rest of the way will be much easier. Experience success no matter how small, every day, to contribute to your piggy bank of self-confidence and motivation and create a huge internal power that will allow you to achieve any goal. For example, if you want to be able to do 100 pushups, increase the number of pushups you do during each training, if you want to learn a foreign language, memorize 10 new words during each class, or if you want to publish a novel, write 1 more page during each writing session. Aim to make small achievements regularly because success breeds success and the more success you experience, the more success you will draw in the future.

Success log and virtual support group

Your internal power that pushes you towards achievement is based on your self-confidence and motivation. Both self-confidence and motivation depend on memories of your past successes and moments when people who you respect believed in you. You can increase your internal power by using the following technique:

Firstly, remember a moment when you successfully achieved a goal that was highly important to you. So important that you were proud of yourself and felt like a rock star. In your imagination see what you saw at that time, hear what you

The Achievement Factory

heard at that time, and feel what you felt at that time. In a few minutes after you have recalled the moment that is associated with this achievement and experienced a feeling of success you felt at that time, your internal power will be increased. Next, repeat the same process with several more memories of your major achievements to increase the internal power even further. There is no moment when you are more motivated to take action and confident that you are capable of achieving any goal than after significant achievement. If you regularly recall past successes, your internal engine will become more powerful and will get you to the goals faster. A great thing to do is to write a list of your major achievements on a sheet of paper and to put it on the wall next to your desk so that when you occasionally look at it you remember what you have accomplished in the past and increase your internal power necessary to accomplish even more in the future.

Secondly, create your imaginary support group that will cheer you on while you take actions that bring you closer to the goal. Recall clearly the people who supported you the most in the past and their most encouraging words and compliments. For example, I remember when my math teacher said, "Andrii, I haven't ever seen anyone as purposeful as you. You are going to have a great future," I remember when my friend said, "Andrii, I believe that you will achieve anything you want," and I remember a guy who, after my presentation, said, "Andrii, it was the best speech I ever heard. I think you will become incredibly successful." All these people are your imaginary support group and they are ready to cheer you up again and again. Whenever you feel depressed or upset, remember people from your support group and the words they said and these memories will increase your self-confidence, motivation and internal power.

After you achieve a big goal or hear words of support from a person you respect, you experience a boost of self-confidence and motivation to make your dreams a reality. Every time you remember your major achievements or the words of the virtual support group, your subconscious believes that those moments are happening right now and as a result you become more self-confident and motivated to achieve your next goal. This technique not only gives extra fuel to your internal engine but also makes the process of goal achievement more enjoyable.

Support of other people in reaching your goal

In my childhood, I loved watching action movies about ninjas, samurais, kung fu and dreamed of learning karate. When my parents presented me with a manual written by Kiokushin Karate founder Masutatsu Oyama, I was on cloud nine and decided, "I will begin training right away!" I read the first 10 pages, tried several karate moves but in an hour got bored to death. I put away the manual and never practiced karate at home after that.

Later my parents enrolled me in the Kiokushin Karate school which I attended four times a week for several years. I not only learned fighting, participated in numerous competitions and received a blue belt, but also enjoyed every hour of training. Why was this approach much more successful than an attempt to learn karate through the book? The answer is —

communication with people. When people talk they exchange not only words but also their energy. Every time you interact with someone and this interaction is positive and relevant to your goal, your internal battery responsible for achieving this goal is charged. When I attended the karate school I listened to the trainer and my internal battery was charged, I interacted with single-minded students who had the same goal as I and my internal battery was charged, I discussed my classes with my parents and my internal battery was charged. My internal energy was high and as a result I had a huge desire to learn karate, trained as hard as I could and also enjoyed the process.

When you want to achieve a big goal, seek interaction with other people as much as possible to charge your internal battery with the necessary energy: find a mentor, talk with single-minded people who want to achieve a similar goal to yours, discuss your progress with friends or relatives, attend conferences, build a mastermind group or communicate on the internet. The more your internal battery is charged, the more motivation you have to achieve a goal, the more productively you act and the greater your success is. To achieve a big goal, you need a lot of energy, and positive communication with people is an excellent energy source that high achievers extensively use and a source of energy that you can't ignore.

Support from others is critical to your success. When you have support, the voices of encouragement soften the negative voices in your head. – Tammy Helfrich

There are two types of people – anchors and motors. You want to lose the anchors and get with the motors because the motors are going somewhere and they're having more fun. The anchors will just drag you down. — Wyland, world-renowned marine artist

Last 5 minutes of the day

Celebrate success and reward yourself

If you recognize all intermediate achievements during the day, you will become more motivated to take action because of the mental connection in your head: "Completing a task means pleasure." Every time you accomplish a step on the way to the goal, celebrate success to draw even more success in future. Celebrating means simply giving yourself pleasure as a reward for work well done.

Firstly, after completing a task, praise yourself, "I am super awesome! Great job!" "You are the man! Keep on going!" or "You are the best! I love you!" Praise is always pleasurable even if you praise yourself. If the task completed was really important, you can even do a winner's dance or brag to your colleague, friend or better half.

Secondly, to recognize completion of the task, you can strike a deal with yourself, "I will do this work now and then I will eat an apple," "I will work consistently for 30 minutes and then I will drink a coffee" or "I will meet this deadline successfully and then I will go for a short walk around the office."

Once I observed how animals are trained to do tricks in a circus. A trainer gives a command and every time an animal fulfills the command correctly, he rewards it with tasty food. After a while the animal fulfills a command correctly almost without failure because it knows, "Completing a command means pleasure." This method works extremely effectively not only for training animals but also for training our own subconscious mind. Reward yourself regularly for successfully completing steps on the way to the goal and you will be super productive in everything you do because of the reflex: "When I complete a task, it's pleasurable. I achieve a goal and I like it!" Celebrating every completed task within a day no matter how small will not only motivate you to work harder but will also make the process of goal achievement more pleasurable.

Daily progress and daily plan

In the evening just before going to bed briefly enter everything you have accomplished within a day into a dedicated computer file or notebook. Even if the task you completed wasn't big or you failed but learned a valuable lesson, write it down to keep track of your achievements. Next, go to the mirror, look yourself in the eyes and praise yourself for every accomplishment you made within a day, passionately and out loud.

Consider every day as a fierce competition against yesterday's you. Ask yourself in the evening: "Did I get at least one step closer to my goal today compared to yesterday?" If the answer is yes, you win this competition and if you win this competition regularly you will achieve any goal sooner than you think. Aim to accomplish the maximum within a day and finish each day successfully because you get closer to your long-term goal by achieving your short-term daily goals.

If you know, "At the end of each day I'll record the results and celebrate the accomplishments," you will be motivated to do as much as possible within a day and as a result will reach a goal sooner. This technique of writing down and celebrating the accomplishments in the evening will help to track what you have done and increase motivation to take action.

In the evening just before going to bed in addition to writing down the results of the day also write down a list of tasks you want to complete tomorrow. If you clearly understand what to do in the morning, you will act without procrastination and focus on tasks that have the biggest impact on how soon you achieve a goal. According to the Dominican University study, people who create a plan and regularly check their results increase their chances of achieving a goal by at least 15%.

You might ask, "Does it matter if I write a plan for the day in the evening of the day before or in the morning?" If you write a list of action items in the evening, your subconscious mind will think the entire night about how to fulfill tasks from the list most effectively. When you sleep your subconscious mind processes thousands of thought combinations and by the time you wake up will generate ideas valuable for accomplishing the tasks. Planning your next day before going to bed is a very effective strategy to increase productivity and subsequent success.

Imagine that you could accomplish only one task tomorrow. Which task would it be so that after the evening review session you would still consider the day more or less successful? Identify the most important task from the list by answering this question, then in the morning concentrate on this task single-mindedly until it's 100% complete. Accomplishment of the most important task will charge your enthusiasm to successfully complete the rest of the tasks from the list and will set the tone for the rest of the day. Creating a plan for the day makes your actions focused; however, if you also specify the most important task from the list that you will accomplish first, you will make your actions laser focused and your time will be spent as effectively as possible.

Before going to bed, spend 5 minutes on summarizing what you have accomplished during the day, celebrating your success and writing down a plan for tomorrow. Although this ritual takes very little time it is one of the most powerful techniques that high achievers use and can increase your productivity and satisfaction from the process of goal achievement multiple times.

Follow effective action with quiet reflection. From the quiet reflection will come even more effective action. – Peter Drucker

The Idea Lifestyle

In order to make your life happier, you need to generate ideas of what exactly you want. Once you have created an idea of what exactly you want, then you need to generate plenty of ideas daily of how to accomplish each particular task on the way to achievement of your goal. After the goal is achieved, you again need to generate ideas of what else you want to achieve and this cycle goes in circles and never ends. As you can see, fulfillment of dreams highly depends on how effectively you can generate ideas and in this section we will discuss three principles that most creative people in the world use and that will help you to generate as many brilliant ideas as you need in the shortest time possible.

Think and Rest

Numerous research studies were conducted to compare the performance of our right brain (subconscious mind) and left brain (conscious mind). The results confirmed that our creative right brain is at least 2 million times faster than our analytical left brain. The analytical left brain is responsible for judging, self-monitoring and internal dialogue. It prevents you from saying everything you think and doing everything you consider. The right brain is responsible for generating new creative ideas. The right brain is responsible for all activities that involve creativity and can process enormous amounts of information within seconds.

Many people think, "In order to generate ideas, I simply need to sit for few hours and think about a problem until I generate one great idea." In fact, this approach rarely gives good results because it contradicts with principles of subconscious thinking. The most effective thinking technique that world-class thinkers use daily is Think and Rest because it allows the subconscious mind to produce successful ideas quickly and with little effort.

Firstly, for 30 minutes, 60 minutes or several hours, think about the problem and how to solve it and write down all ideas that come to your mind, no matter how crazy they are. Aim to generate as many ideas as possible because in the world of creativity quantity equals quality and the more ideas you generate, the higher chances are that one of them will be brilliant. During this initial thinking stage you not only generate ideas but also let your subconscious mind know which ideas you need. If your problem is simple, you may find a good solution already during this initial brainstorming session, but if you don't find an appropriate solution within the first several hours, forget about your problem completely and get back to your everyday life.

Secondly, after you stop thinking about the problem consciously, your subconscious will continue thinking about it 24/7. When you think about the problem you give your subconscious mind a command, "I am interested in finding a solution for this problem. Please generate ideas for me." After the subconscious mind receives a command during the time when you don't consciously focus on the problem, it makes random connections between millions of thoughts in the back of your mind and once it sees that one of the connections seems interesting says, "Hey, here is one more good idea for you." The subconscious mind generates most of your best ideas after you have forgotten about the problem and during moments you least expect them. Whether an idea pops into your head while you are in the shower, waiting in line or falling asleep – write it down instantly.

Finally, think about your problem occasionally for 2 to 5 minutes. During this time, you will not only generate fresh ideas but will also reactivate your creative mind and make it think intensively while you are not consciously thinking about the problem. The difference between days when you generate plenty of excellent ideas and days when you generate zero ideas is simply whether you gave your subconscious mind a task or not. Thinking about a problem for a few minutes several times during the day will make your subconscious mind work intensively on the problem 24/7 and generate excellent ideas in abundance. The subconscious mind is especially productive while you sleep because it isn't blocked by the analytical brain, that's why it will be very rewarding if one of the times you think about the problem is before you go to bed. Just 10 to 15 minutes of thinking a day about your tasks is more than enough to activate your subconscious mind to work on ideas and to turn your dreams into reality.

The Think and Rest technique doesn't take much time; however, it activates the subconscious mind and makes it think about the problem day and night and as a result generates valuable ideas as productively as possible. The Think and Rest technique helps the best innovators and thinkers to generate successful ideas in 100% of cases. If after using this technique a great idea still doesn't come to you, it means that either not enough time has passed or your subconscious mind doesn't have enough raw materials to create ideas from. You might ask, "What are raw materials for creativity?" About that in the next section…

I have found, for example, that if I have to write upon some rather difficult topic, the best plan is to think about it with very great intensity — the greatest intensity of which I am capable — for a few hours or days, and at the end of that time give orders, so to speak (to my subconscious mind) that the work is to proceed underground. After some months I return consciously to the topic and find that the work has been done. — Bertrand Russell, the British logician and mathematician

Expose yourself to new experiences

One day little Jimmy went to his best friend Suzy's house and noticed the beautiful constructions she built from a Lego set. He looked at cars, ships and castles and decided, "I want to build beautiful Lego constructions, too."

Jimmy took two little pieces of a Lego set that he owned. He spent hours looking at them and trying to put them together in all possible combinations but realized that no matter what he did these 2 pieces never looked like a car, a ship or a castle. He went to Suzy and said, "Suzy, I am just not creative enough to build beautiful Lego constructions." Suzy looked at him, smiled and said, "Jimmy, you have the talent to create beautiful Lego constructions. You just don't have enough constructor pieces. I have been collecting my Lego pieces for years and now have thousands of them. If you had as many pieces as I do, you would easily create even better constructions."

Ideas are combinations of other ideas and the more diverse life experiences you have, the more different ideas you will be able to construct. Many people say, "I can't create great business ideas. I am not creative." However, the true reason why they fail is that they have too few different experiences in their memory to construct new ideas from.

The world's greatest thinkers have an insatiable curiosity and actively seek new experiences that can increase the amount of their creative constructor pieces. They travel, make new acquaintances, try various hobbies, attend conferences and seminars, and read books, magazines and blogs. In the world of creativity, the wealthy person is not the one who has more money but the one who has more experiences to build ideas from.

People whose life follows the same pattern for years may find themselves in a situation like little Jimmy who tried to create something incredible from just several pieces of a Lego set. Constantly bombard your brain with new ideas and experiences which will become raw materials for your future successful ideas. The more different experiences you have had in life, the more ideas of others you have learned, the more creative combinations your brain will be able to make and the more valuable ideas it will generate. If you want to be a world-class thinker, a quest for new creative raw materials should become your habit.

Creativity is just connecting things. When you ask creative people how they did something, they feel a little guilty because they didn't really do it, they just saw something. It seemed obvious to them after a while. That's because they were able to connect experiences they've had and synthesize new things. And the reason they were able to do that was that they've had more experiences or they have thought more about their experiences than other people. Unfortunately, that's too rare a commodity. A lot of people in our industry haven't had very diverse experiences. So they don't have enough dots to connect, and they end up with very linear solutions without a broad perspective on the problem. – Steve Jobs

I really had a lot of dreams when I was a kid, and I think a great deal of that grew out of the fact that I had a chance to read a lot. – Bill Gates

Train creative muscles

When I was in 7th grade, my math teacher Alexander said to my mother, "Victoria, your son's performance is very poor. Honestly, I think math isn't his thing. It would be better for Andrii if you transfer him to another school at the end of the year." My classmate Peter was a naturally gifted student and several heads above everyone I knew at math. He always solved problems nobody else could and Alexander called him "math heavy artillery."

In 8th grade, after one incident in class I became very interested in math. I began devoting all my spare time to math and by the end of the year became the second-best math student in the class after Peter. In 9th grade, Peter became very interested in guitar, founded his own band and neglected math. By the end of the 9th grade, I outperformed Peter and became the strongest math student in the entire school. In 10th grade, I continued devoting at least 4 hours a day to solving problems and by the end of the year became one of the 100 best math students in the Ukraine.

Peter is certainly much more gifted than I am, but I trained significantly more. I am sure that if he devoted at least half the time that I did to math he would achieve far better results than I. If you are interested to know what happened to Peter later, he became a guitar player in one of the most popular bands in the Ukraine.

When people see a person who can do 100 pushups they don't say, "Wow this person was born with a gift to do pushups. Unfortunately, I don't have a talent for pushups and will never be able to do as many pushups as he (or she)." Everybody knows that if you want to be able to do 100 pushups you simply need to develop your chest muscles by doing pushups regularly for several months. It's a common belief that people who can generate excellent ideas quickly have a special talent, however in reality these people just have bigger creative muscles because they think about ideas more often than others. If you practice generating ideas regularly, after some time your creative muscles will become stronger, your subconscious will process random combinations of thoughts faster and you will produce better ideas than the majority of naturally gifted people.

Many people rarely give tasks to their subconscious mind and as a result when they realize that their creative muscles are weak say, "I just don't have talent for creating ideas." This sounds the same as, "I exercise only twice a year and can't do more than 5 pushups. I don't have the talent for pushups."

The more you practice pushups, the more pushups you will be able to do. The same happens with ideas. The more you practice creative thinking, the quicker high-quality ideas will come to your mind. If you take practicing idea generation seriously, in a few years your creative muscles will be so strong that other people may call you a creative genius.

The Achievement Factory

Certainly, every child is born blessed with a vivid imagination. But just as muscles grow flabby with disuse, so the bright imagination of a child pales in later years if he ceases to exercise it. — Walt Disney

If you want to make your life an exciting adventure, ideas should become your lifestyle. If you have an "idea lifestyle," you first generate ideas about what you want, then you generate ideas about how to achieve what you want and finally you take actions and achieve it. The life experiences you gained on the way to achievement of the goal will serve as valuable raw material for creating new desirable goals and for even greater quality ideas of how to achieve these new goals. And this sequence will go in circles over and over again. The more ideas you generate, the more goals you set and achieve, the more experiences you have, the bigger creative muscles you build and these lead to even more ideas.

The quantity and quality of ideas that you create are essential for goal achievement and once you make ideas your lifestyle, they will come to you much more often because your creative muscles will be stronger and your creative constructor will have more pieces. Once you make the idea lifestyle your lifestyle, become obsessed about ideas and make them one of your core values, you will succeed in all areas of life, fulfill all your dreams and make your life an exciting adventure.

All achievements, all earned riches, have their beginning in an idea. — Napoleon Hill, American self-help guru

Final Checklist

Before we get to the end of the book I want you to give yourself a present. Complete a "100 dreams" exercise and choose one dream from the list, fulfillment of which will bring you the biggest joy. Make a commitment to fulfill this dream and take the first step towards living a life of your dreams right now. All of the information in *The Achievement Factory* may help you to achieve goals more effectively, however let me remind you of the five core foundations that you might use for achievement of the dream you have chosen most often.

1. Set a specific and measurable goal

This step might take you just a few minutes, however it might have the biggest impact on whether you achieve your dream or not. Formulate your dream as a specific and measurable goal to set a direction for your actions clearly. The more specific and measurable a goal is, the more precise and impactful will be your actions and the sooner your dream will become a reality.

2. Visualize a goal

Visualization is one of the most powerful techniques that high achievers use to fulfill their dreams because it is incredibly effective. Visualization allows you to increase your desire to achieve a goal, to activate the subconscious to generate valuable ideas, to increase focus and to set an internal filter to notice relevant resources. The visualization magic formula says clarity of visualization X regularity of visualization = achieved goal.

3. Last 5 minutes of the day

At the end of each day check the progress you have made during the day and celebrate success. Also, set a plan of what you want to accomplish tomorrow. This short ritual will make you more motivated to take actions, will make each of your days more productive and will make the path towards achievement of the goal shorter.

4. Think and Rest

The subconscious mind (the creative brain) is responsible for generating ideas and ideas are essential for achievement of any goal. The subconscious mind stays idle if you don't activate it by giving it problems to solve. Use the Think and Rest technique daily to keep the subconscious mind thinking about how to achieve a goal most effectively and you will get excellent ideas in abundance. Every time a great idea comes to your mind, evaluate it and if it can help you to achieve a goal add it to your action plan.

5. Take massive action

Of course in order to achieve a goal you need to take massive action. In terms of actions two things are important to remember. Focus your attention as much as possible on the goal, because the longer you focus on the goal within a day, the more actions you take. Secondly, remember that according to the Law of Inertia it's very difficult to begin taking actions, but once you have overcome the initial resistance you will be taking massive action daily with pleasure and without much effort.

The Achievement Factory

After fulfilling this dream, give yourself presents regularly and your life will always be happy and full of exciting adventures. Remember that you can achieve anything you want if you have a desire and make a commitment. Repeat after me, "My life is in my hands. I promise to live happily and fulfill all my dreams no matter how big they are." Now you have your own Achievement Factory that, if managed properly, will make your life an exciting adventure.

The poorest man in the world is the man without a dream. The most frustrated man in the world is the man with a dream that never becomes reality. – Myles Munroe

What to read next?

If you liked this book, you will also like *The Business Idea Factory: A World-Class System for Creating Successful Business Ideas*. Principles described in this book will allow you to effectively create successful business ideas and make your life more adventurous.

Another interesting book is *Magic of Impromptu Speaking: Create a Speech That Will Be Remembered for Years in Under 30 Seconds*. In this book, you will learn how to be in the moment, speak without preparation and always find the right words when you need them.

I also highly recommend you to read *Magic of Public Speaking: A Complete System to Become a World Class Speaker*. By using this system, you can unleash your public speaking potential in a very short period of time.

Biography

At the age of 19, Andrii obtained his CCIE (Certified Cisco Internetwork Expert) certification, the most respected certification in the IT world, and became the youngest person in Europe to hold it.

At the age of 23, he joined an MBA program at one of the top 10 MBA schools in the USA as the youngest student in the program, and at the age of 25 he joined Cisco Systems' Head Office as a Product Manager responsible for managing a router which brought in $1 billion in revenue every year.

These and other experiences have taught Andrii that success in any endeavor doesn't as much depend on the amount of experience you have but rather on the processes that you are using. Having dedicated over 10 years to researching behavior of world's most successful people and testing a variety of different techniques, Andrii has uncovered principles that will help you to unleash your potential and fulfill your dreams in a very short period of time.

The Business Idea Factory

A World-Class System for Creating Successful Business Ideas

The Business Idea Factory is an effective and easy-to-use system for creating successful business ideas. It is based on 10 years of research into idea-generation techniques used by the world's best scientists, artists, CEOs, entrepreneurs and innovators. The book is entertaining to read, has plenty of stories and offers bits of wisdom necessary to increase the quantity and quality of ideas that you create multiple times. Once you begin applying strategies described in this book, you will create successful business ideas regularly and make your life more adventurous. You will realize that there are few things that can bring as much joy and success in business as the moment when an excellent idea comes to your head.

Magic of Impromptu Speaking

Create a Speech That Will Be Remembered for Years in Under 30 Seconds

Magic of Impromptu Speaking is a comprehensive, step-by-step system for creating highly effective speeches in under 30 seconds. It is based on research of the most powerful techniques used by winners of impromptu speaking contests, politicians, actors and successful presenters. The book is entertaining to read, has plenty of examples and covers the most effective tools not only from the world of impromptu speaking but also from acting, stand-up comedy, applied psychology and creative thinking.

Once you master the system, you will grow immensely as an impromptu public speaker, become a better storyteller in a circle of friends and be more creative in everyday life. Your audience members will think that what you do on stage after such short preparation is pure magic and will recall some of your speeches many years later.

Magic of Public Speaking

A Complete System to Become a World Class Speaker

The Magic of Public Speaking is a comprehensive step-by-step system for creating highly effective speeches. It is based on research from the top 1000 speakers in the modern world. The techniques you will learn have been tested on hundreds of professional speakers and work! You will receive the exact steps needed to create a speech that will keep your audience on the edge of their seats. The book is easy to follow, entertaining to read and uses many examples from real speeches. This system will make sure that every time you go on stage your speech is an outstanding one.

Printed in Great Britain
by Amazon